A PSYCHIC'S CASEBOOK

A PSYCHIC'S CASEBOOK

Dilys Gater

Chivers Press • Thorndike Press
Bath, England   Thorndike, Maine USA

This Large Print edition is published by Chivers Press, England, and by Thorndike Press, USA.

Published in 1998 in the U.K. by arrangement with Robert Hale Ltd.

Published in 1998 in the U.S. by arrangement with Robert Hale Ltd.

U.K. Hardcover ISBN 0–7540–3113–6 (Chivers Large Print)
U.S. Softcover   ISBN 0–7862–1227–6 (General Series Edition)

The text of this Large Print edition is unabridged.
Other aspects of the book may vary from the original edition.

Set in 16 pt. New Times Roman.

Printed in Great Britain on acid-free paper.

British Library Cataloguing in Publication Data available

Library of Congress Cataloging-in-Publication Data

Gater, Dilys.
  A psychic's casebook / Dilys Gater.
    p. cm.
  Originally published: 1995.
  ISBN 0–7862–1227–6 (large print : sc : alk. paper)
    1. Gater, Dilys. 2. Psychics—United States—Biography.
BF1027.G37A3   1998
133.8′.092—dc21

97–28640

CONTENTS

Foreword by Richard Lawler   ix

 1 Psychic at Work   1
 2 Voices from the Other Side   20
 3 Contact with Past Lives   44
 4 Lost, Haunted, Possessed   64
 5 Seeing Clear   87
 6 Angels, Aliens and Star Children   105
 7 In Touch   125
 8 The Gift of Healing   145
 9 Written in the Cards   165
10 Achievement   182

Sorcerer's Apprentice—A Brief Guide for
   New and Aspiring Psychics   202
Selected Books Recommended to Sitters   218

To Astra, who showed me my first miracle
To DHS, thank you for the blossoms
still fresh after twenty years
To Richard who gave me confidence,
inspiration and a crown of stars
And to my fellow travellers along the
Ancient and Shining Way
Notta—Good Will

'Do you do healing, incidentally? You give off a lot of blue colour—you do have a lot of blue colour—it's there, it's part of what you are, what you have grown into in this life. You show me blue—a healing colour. We cannot give off a colour that we are not—you are vibrating at that force. And you say "I have power"—yes, you have—power is the same vibrating force. But remember the body, the personality, everything you are now, is totally temporary, it is not reality. The reality is the power.'

*Medium Mary Absalom in trance
to Dilys Gater,
Recorded at the College of Psychic Studies,
London, April 1993.*

FOREWORD

Richard Lawler
Astrologer, psychic, lecturer, advanced master

Years ago, when running a channelling group, as well as various god-forms, we were occasionally informed of enlightened earthly beings who would flower in the future. When I gave talks in the Arthur Conan Doyle Room at Belgrave Square, the writer himself often came through and said:
'D ... s will be a better writer than me.' On another occasion he added: 'Holmes could learn a thing or two from her.'

Doris Stokes told me that she liked Katrina Wright's novels (Katrina Wright is one of Gater's pseudonyms)—they lifted her spirits after contacting 'dead' children. When I was organizing her first public 'gig' in the Parkway Cinema in Camden, she revealed: 'My guides have told me that I will be succeeded by a lady with the same number of letters in her first name as mine'. In Fulham, at the Old Town Hall development group, she told me that, 'My successor will have the same first initial as me.' In Wandsworth she remarked once: 'They have told me that my spiritual heiress will have the same last letter in her name as me.'

'Well, Dr Watson, the real D ... s is here.'

'I think your brain is phenomenal, Holmes.'
'I will confirm that,' agreed Dr Finlay, at the opening of the New Psychic Group at the London Spiritual Mission in 1976. 'It will be a Greater World with Gater in our world.'

Richard Lawler

Note: The Arthur Finlay College, Stansted, named for a well known figure in spiritual history, is familiar to all those interested or involved in the psychic world.

CHAPTER ONE

PSYCHIC AT WORK

I am a practising psychic. That is, I possess certain powers which I am able to use for the benefit of others, and I spend quite a lot of my time employing these powers in this way. This is how most professional psychics work. There are very few who skulk mysteriously in dimly lit rooms, clad in robes with magical symbols on them, and muttering incomprehensible names of spirits. A psychic today is respectable, a consultant who is, in the same way as a doctor or a psychiatrist, available for consultation. Patients, sitters—whatever you like to call them—come to a psychic for different 'treatment', but generally their need is the same—encouragement, sympathy, an easing of pain, light in the darkness, a sense that troubles will not go on for ever, reassurance that there is some purpose to it all, guidance both physical and spiritual, and loving human contact, feeling that somebody cares.

As a psychic, I have found that the cases of people who come to me are many and varied. Often they are just as drastic as the sort of thing a doctor might consider an emergency. One young woman at a psychic fair I attended, hung round my table for a long time, watching other people having readings, holding back, hesitating. She was dressed in black leather, and seemed very sure of herself, so much so that strong men would probably have thought twice before even cracking a male chauvinistic joke. At last, after about two hours, she approached when I was free, and sat down, seemingly very much in control.

As usual, I began the sitting by asking her to let me hold her hands, and tell me her name, which was Helen. Immediately I picked up what I had already previously suspected.

'You're very depressed, aren't you? You look tough, as though nothing can get to you, but I'm feeling a terrible blackness, a sense of alienation and hurt, a lot of pain.'

She gave me a look then spoke briefly. 'Yes.'

'You're thinking—considering—you have been thinking of trying to do something desperate.'

She gave a shaky sigh and her voice was suddenly vulnerable as those desperately clutched-at defences crumbled.

'Last night I—nearly did—I just—hung on—but I don't know how long I can.'

As I held her hands I knew why I had been guided to the fair that day. All sitters are equally important, but with Helen it was literally a matter of life and death. She had come to me to save her, to draw her back into the world, to be the channel through which she could find the courage to face life again. Sometimes, in that situation, it is enough for the right person to be there at the right time, in the right place—the psychic powers make it just that much easier for the psychic to provide what is needed.

Helen was even able to summon a goodbye smile as she eventually left. I gave her my telephone number and told her to ring me at any time if she needed to talk, as I do to all sitters. Most never ring back—and the ones who do generally want to tell me, breathlessly, of how some seemingly miraculous happening has occurred or how much better things have been.

Denise, an elderly friend, did not consult me formally, but, as we talked on the phone, she told me about her dilemma in choosing whether to leave the house where she and her husband were living and retire to a more idyllic cottage, or to stay put. I asked whether the house where she lived had a garden—yes, it did—and then whether she would be able to plant some lilies of the valley which need shade and coolness.

Denise replied immediately that there was a huge bed of lilies of the valley in the back garden already, and I knew the answer to her problem.

'That is where you should stay.'

I could not have explained why, all I knew clairvoyantly was that she must be near that particular flower. But about six months later she phoned me again, in great excitement.

'You know you told me we should stay here—and you were so right, we can see that now. I have very high blood pressure and I think I might not have survived a big move—well, I'm reading a book about the Victorians, and you'll never believe this—but the Victorians used to use lily of the valley to treat high blood pressure medically. And you said I should stay where they were—isn't that amazing?'

I agreed that it was, but the time has long passed since I was taken off balance by the power, strength and wisdom of the messages I am given psychically, the images that I receive through clairvoyance, the seemingly odd guidelines the spiritual world applies through me to problems that can range from potential suicide to all aspects of love—including homosexual and lesbian lovers—and the passionate grief of the bereaved. Women who want children, women who want husbands, women who want to be free to be themselves, men who are troubled, hurt, tired, unfulfilled—they come to the psychic hopefully, wanting a miracle. And as a psychic, I have seen miracles happen. They happen every day—but often not in the way the recipient expects.

Psychics are not necessarily spiritual or mystical people. Their powers become as

4

familiar to them as the five senses are to everyone else. They also learn how to 'switch off' so that they are not always, as it were, on duty. Using psychic energy can be tiring and draining, so psychics work semi-regular hours, as other people do. They can be consulted anywhere, at any time, if necessary, but their work is largely done in their homes (or visiting the homes of sitters), in healing centres or places given over to psychic activity, or at psychic fairs.

Psychic fairs are held everywhere, all through the year, and involve a day, evening or weekend, where visitors can have their tarot cards read, consult a medium, hear about the past, present and future, purchase gem stones or crystals, be spiritually comforted—and have a cup of tea while listening to lectures or watching a demonstration. In someone's home, there is privacy and a feeling of security. At a centre or fair, the concentration of psychic and spiritual energy helps to create an atmosphere conducive to harmony, peace and calm. But a psychic may be required to work anywhere, even in the most unlikely places.

A dear friend of mine, Wanda, suffers from a drastic wasting disease, and has bravely faced nineteen operations on her eyes within the last five years. Every time I see her, she is the same—full of optimism and vitality, pursuing the new career she took up as her sight and strength began to flag, that of a writer. We had not seen one another for many months because of the deterioration of her sight, and when we were able to meet up, it had to be at a 'mid-way' point easy to get to. We met at McDonalds in Wimbledon!

She was anxious to have a reading, but there was nowhere to go. So, with a background of piped music, orders for Big Macs and shakes, laughter and occasional roars from the children, and the buzz of gossiping coffee-drinkers, I took her hands across the table alongside our polystyrene coffee beakers and let the light and the power come through. Not only clairvoyant messages and visions for the future, but healing too was there in abundance even in surroundings as unlikely as those.

*   *   *

What exactly are the powers possessed by a psychic? They vary from person to person, so I will be talking in this book about those I possess myself, and the methods I employ in my work, which may not be the same as those used by other psychics. All aim though—or should aim—for the same results: spiritual growth, upliftment, positivity. Psychics are not—or should not be—entertainers, only, if they have to be, in passing. They have been given their gifts to use for the benefit of others, not for their own ego-tripping or to make a lot of money from an 'act'. There are many cases of psychics who have let the material side, personal importance, money or fame, go to their heads, and the result is inevitably the same—the powers, if misused, are withdrawn.

Everyone is psychic, but not all to the same degree. Psychic powers are like the popular idea of the 'third eye', always there but only able to be used if recognized and practised in use in the same way as our physical sight, hearing or other senses. There are some people who will never be psychically sensitive, while many more are unaware of their potential. Others may know they have the power, but they are frightened or for some other reason choose to ignore it. Often, people who come to me are looking for practical advice, assistance in developing their abilities.

The word 'psychic' means a person 'considered to have occult powers, such as telepathy, clairvoyance, etc.' Psychic phenomena are those 'inexplicable by natural laws'. The word 'occult' means concealed, secret, mystical, magical. But it is only in the popular press and in the minds of those who do not bother to look at the facts, that 'psychic' can become a byword for 'frightening' or 'fake', or even, on occasion, 'forbidden' and 'evil'.

The powers of psychics can be backed up—usually in complicated language—by such erudite and respected criteria as the theories of mathematics and quantum physics, as well as by psychiatry and medicine. And, like a gift for mathematics or quantum physics, the gift of psychic power is neither good nor bad, it is simply there. Everything depends on the way it is used.

My own powers are inherent and intuitive and have been developing (largely without my conscious awareness) throughout the whole of my life. The cases detailed in this book are genuine not generalised, but all names have been changed to protect the confidentiality of my sitters, and the stage name under which I work has been withheld for extra privacy for those mentioned here. Where quotes have been used it is with the permission of the writers.

Vera, a lady in her mid-sixties, confided to me how unhappy she was because of difficulties in her life-long friendship with Arda, who had achieved greater success than herself in the career they both shared— broadcasting and lecturing. Though Arda was more successful, she clung to her 'best friend' of so many years for constant reassurance, often at the expense of Vera's own needs. As a result, Vera felt the friendship had changed, and the time had come for her to withdraw herself a certain amount from Arda to attend to her own fragile creative ego and her own more modest ambitions. But the situation was emotional for her, and she was feeling hurt and upset.

I told her that, to help her deal with this

situation, she should buy some white arum lilies—funeral flowers—and keep them near her in a vase whenever she and Arda were together, preferably directly between the two of them. What had happened was that she had 'lost' someone, the person she had so loyally loved, supported and relied on herself for so long. Over the years, Arda had changed, the relationship had changed, and Vera needed to recognize the change by mourning the loss of what had passed.

I told her that the presence of the flowers in physical recognition of her 'loss' would give her a sense of distance from the powerful personality of her friend, and enable her to keep her dignity and her sense of self. The consciousness of mourning for what had gone would make it easier for her to settle the new, more positive pattern their friendship would take in the future.

As with the case of Denise and her lilies of the valley, this advice, given to me clairvoyantly, worked. Vera reported that the presence of the white lilies had indeed given her a 'breathing space' and a chance to find her feet again when she was with Arda. No doubt a psychiatrist could explain exactly how the result came about, but the spirits who are responsible for true clairvoyance never feel the need for explanations. And they are always right.

*   *   *

As a psychic, I am able to practise many of the psychic powers. The most difficult to quantify is that of clairvoyance. This means, literally, being able to 'see' things which are not in front of your eyes—for instance, being able to 'pick up' (my own words) places, things and people you have never physically seen or met, being able to describe them, and being able to know what the people are thinking or feeling. Sitters often ask whether their husband or boyfriend (not so often the other way about) is having an affair with someone else; whether their children (or parents) on the other side of the world are all right; or whether the person they have met will prove to be their true love.

*   *   *

One of the saddest cases I have ever dealt with of this type was a lady called Theresa, who came to me, small but determined, at a psychic fair, and said bluntly that after a lifetime of cheating on her with a mistress called Priscilla (she gave me the lady's full name and details) her husband was about to get his comeuppance. She and her husband were about to retire and due for enormous 'golden handshakes' from the firm they both worked for. But Theresa was laying her plans to divorce her man, claim a half of everything, and retire to the sun. She wanted to consult me on the advisability of calling in private detectives to collect evidence for a divorce now, or waiting until the 'handshakes' were safely in the bank.

When I picked up her husband, checking on the true state of affairs, I saw that in spite of Theresa's conviction, which had ruined the best part of her married life and taken away all her pleasures except the prospect of 'revenge', he had never been unfaithful to her at all. I picked up the girlfriend also and verified that she was just that—a friend. The whole thing had only existed in Theresa's mind, and I knew that private detectives would soon tell her so if they were called in.

I tried to suggest that it might be wise to know the truth, even if, perhaps, her husband was innocent, but she assured me categorically there was no chance of that. Though he had tried to pretend there was nothing in it, she said, she knew the evidence would be there, and was determined to make sure he got what was coming to him.

In psychic work, it cannot be said too many times that there is always a right time, with the right person in the right place. I knew this was not the time to try to change Theresa. One cannot undo the realities people build around themselves in a lifetime, unless they genuinely want to change. Even then, growing, spiritually or mentally, can prove painful and must be undertaken in the utmost sincerity and commitment, with full awareness. In Theresa's case, she did not even recognize how far removed her own reality was from the truth, so I gave her what she was really looking for that evening—a sympathetic ear, a feeling things would improve and that there was something better ahead for her, and a reassurance that she mattered and her life had not been a waste. She left telling me she felt much better and was going to call the detectives the next day. But somehow, I doubted it. It would have upset her permanent state of betrayal, revenge and plotting about 'the day when', which was the only way of life she had unhappily known for many years. In her case, the time was not ripe—and perhaps, unless she was prepared to face the shock of the truth, her husband's faithfulness, might never be.

*   *   *

Clairvoyance underlines all other powers if you possess it. For instance, many people who are not psychic can give readings of the tarot cards or interpret the lines on the hand or the secrets of the stars. One does not have to be psychic to be a palmist, an astrologer or even what is called a 'tarot reader'. These are skills which—however generally speaking—can be learned from a book, since there are rules and guidelines to follow. The cards, the stars and

12

the palm all give their own messages, including indications of what will happen in the future, without anything clairvoyant being involved.

What clairvoyance does is to add to or even bypass this kind of formal knowledge, though the result is invariably the same. I have a friend whose astrological knowledge and skill has been built up over more than thirty years. Sometimes we look together at an astrological chart which means nothing to me in terms of interpreting the lines on it, but I 'see' with my mind the personality of the person it has been drawn up for, their problems and fears, their past, present and probable future. I ask the astrologer who has been working on it whether I am correct—he always confirms that I have 'seen' the same picture, more or less, that the science of astrology has outlined on the astrological chart.

This phenomenon explains why so many people, even some who are not psychic or clairvoyant at all, claim to be able to foretell the future—and quite often can do so with astounding accuracy. The future is contained in the 'map of life' we each carry written on our hand, or in the patterns of our natal stars and planets. It is revealed too in the spread of the tarot cards. A skilled worker in any of these fields will probably be able to foretell the future to a certain degree without any help from clairvoyance.

But clairvoyance enables me, personally, to

13

be able to see the potential rather than the actual, and to show sitters how they can change the future that seems to loom. Alongside this I work with the gift of healing—whatever form this may take. Sometimes it involves actually healing illness, pain and tension, allaying fear and providing love and support so that sitters can go away with a new strength and confidence in themselves.

One case in particular which summed up all the 'small miracles' of this sort that I have been privileged to witness was that of Marie. She turned up unexpectedly on an autumn afternoon, a slight young woman about five feet tall, drably dressed, with an air of hopelessness, despair and incredible tiredness. I could see the drudgery and lack of affection of her life without even holding her hands or asking questions. She was at the end of her resources, she had given all she had and received no reward, no love or care, not even a thank you. She had nothing and no expectation of anything at all. There was no hope left in her, and she did not know where to turn for money, work, companionship or even the strength to carry on.

I spoke to her in the ways I will be describing later in this book, and gave her healing. She broke down not because things were tough— she could take cruelty without blinking an eye, she was used to it—but because somebody was being kind, treating her with love and concern, caring about her as though she mattered. By the time she left me, with the usual instruction to contact me if she needed me, nothing had been altered in her situation, except that she had been given strength, healing and the will to go forward. She was not a person of many words—but she said she would be 'all right' and I watched her go hoping this would be so.

The miraculous part happened about six months later, when I looked up in the place where I was working and saw her walking towards me—but what a difference. Now she seemed to stand six feet tall, not her own tiny height. Behind her, a pace to the rear, carrying a shopping basket, was a good-looking young man with an infectious twinkling grin. Her hair was glossy and her skin had lost its sallow, sick appearance. She was beaming me a smile that looked very like that of the cat that had got the cream.

She had come to thank me. After her sitting when we had talked, she said she had made a big effort to change the negativity of her life. And things had just fallen miraculously into place. Her whole world had changed. Before she had had nothing, and would have sold her soul for a kind word or the chance to scrub steps. Now she had a good job—as house-keeper at a hotel. She had longed for love—now she had a boyfriend, the young man I had seen, who had taken himself off for a cup of coffee while we talked. They were planning to marry in the summer.

I was able to assure her that the marriage would be a success and that she had found a person worthy of her love. The change in her was incredible, but when she thanked me, I assured her that I was not responsible—she had done it all herself. The potential had been there always, but she had been so badly damaged that she had been unable to see it or reach it. This, to me, is what healing is so often about. Helping people to find a way— sometimes to find themselves.

*　　*　　*

When a psychic makes use of something physical and 'real' like a crystal ball, a pack of cards or rune stones, the objects may be only a means of focusing clairvoyance—though as we have already seen, cards or rune stones or any other system of divination which has its own language and its own rules can also be used by non-psychics. I started off with no knowledge of the tarot and have never studied 'what the cards mean', though after a long time working with psychics, I have picked up quite a lot of the theory. But I have never felt any need to study the formal meanings of the cards (there are 78 of them in a tarot pack, a lot of information to learn) nor the classic 'spreads' and what they mean.

When I do a reading with the cards, I lay

them out in my own personal 'spreads', and I read them according to what I see clairvoyantly in each card, what the pictures say to me in that particular circumstance, rather than by what the rule-book dictates. Since I do many readings, I do find that the same cards usually tell me the same thing—and the meaning is, as with astrology, generally the same as the traditional meaning as taught by Tarot Schools. But in many cases, what I see clairvoyantly will override the traditional meaning of a card.

On one occasion when reading for a young woman who was worrying about her relationship with her boyfriend, I was staring at a familiar card that generally indicates something innocuous like job satisfaction or artistic talent (it was so ordinary that I cannot even recall the card). But rather than commenting on his job satisfaction or whatever it was, I found myself saying, in the middle of the discreet suburban hall where the psychic fair was being held:

'It's because he's a witch, isn't it? He's into witchcraft and that frightens you.'

Her reaction was equally out of the ordinary. Instead of dismissing the idea as ridiculous, (as the average person might expect) she stared then said quietly:

'Well—you're right, actually. I don't know how you knew—I haven't told anybody—he wants me to go and join in and I—well, I do feel frightened. I don't want anything to do with black magic.'

I was able to reassure her that there was nothing to fear. Genuine Wicca, known to the uninitiated as witchcraft, is nothing to do with black magic. It is a discipline of living and celebration of life, a form of worship of nature and the Earth Goddess. Even if she went along, she would find nothing to hurt her—but I felt her boyfriend was probably not a serious convert to Wicca, simply a person with wide ranging interests and more than his share of curiosity about everything under the sun, looking for his own individual way forward. He could well be a Buddhist in six months, I told her, and she smiled reluctantly.

'Yes, that does sound like him.'

She left comforted—but the sudden message about his 'witchcraft' in the cards was just as clairvoyant as on another occasion when I had turned up some other equally ordinary card, but something prompted me to ask my sitter whether she knew a postman—not a person in the sorting office, or a Post Office employee, but a postman.

She replied hesitantly that she had just met someone she liked who was working as a part-time postman—she didn't know him well yet, but—.

'You will,' I said. 'You're going to marry him and be very happy.'

As well as being a clairvoyant, I practise psychometry, which means being able to pick up vibrations from objects and 'tune in' to their owners. Rings or other pieces of jewellery can reveal much about the person who owns them—or, if they are dead, used to own them. From a human hair the personality of the man or woman it belongs to can reveal many secrets. I can pick up information in this way from a photograph—though I do not usually need a picture now, the ability to pick up a person merely by concentrating on their name (which is again composed of a series of vibrations on the ether) will usually accomplish what is necessary.

I also practise as a medium, which means I can contact and communicate with the dead. Not all psychics or clairvoyants are mediums—and equally, not all mediums are clairvoyants. The word medium means a 'channel'—a bridge between the physical world and that of the spirit.

I regard all my psychic work as some form of making contact. Psychics can, most spectacularly, make contact with the dead; they can make contact with previous incarnations and past lives; they can make contact with the future. But a great deal of the work I do is far more subtle. Many people are in distress or despair because they have lost contact with their own selves—with what psychiatrists refer to as their inner child—or with their potential. They have lost contact with the fact that they have a choice, they have a life of their own. A great deal of the misery in the world springs from the darkness of ignorance and fear, and the psychic's powers are given to help combat this darkness with the light of positivity, enlightenment and love.

CHAPTER TWO

VOICES FROM THE OTHER SIDE

Janette arrived at this particular venue with a woman friend, who went to have a reading with someone else. When she hesitantly came to me—a slender girl with long blonde hair, wearing blue jeans and a T-shirt—the place was so crowded that we had to sit in a corner beside a bare office desk. No table tastefully decorated with a cloth, flowers and items like my amethyst bird, 'celestial' cat or the box of semi-precious stones, rose quartz, turquoise, tourmaline, agate, aventurine and lapis lazuli, which I sometimes use in my work, to colour the air like rare blossoms.

We sat down. I took Janette's hands.

'You have very recently suffered a great loss.'

She nodded.

'Who was it? Your boyfriend?'

'No—well, it was a boy, and he was a friend,' she said, with a faint little smile. 'I—I loved him. He didn't think of me as anything except one of the rest of us, but—I—'.

'He was killed, wasn't he? He was very young—and it was very sudden.'

She bit her lip until it was white. 'A car crash. Two weeks ago.'

Her large eyes pleaded with me. She knew I was a medium, but she would not ask in so many words. Often, whether for fear of being disappointed, or because they think it is something they have no right to ask, sitters are reluctant to approach the matter of contacting the dead, and wait for the medium to make the way easy for them.

'You'd like me to try and speak to him?'

'Could you?' Her voice was thin and breathy. 'I just want to know—that he is—all right. I mean, he might be surprised it's me, he didn't take me seriously—'.

I gently stopped her.

'Never mind that. You loved him very much, and his death has caused you suffering. Wherever or whoever it comes from, love is something we all ought to take very seriously. He is safe now, nothing can harm him any more, it is your pain we have to deal with. Let me have his name.'

'Jamie,' she whispered, and we sat with

21

hands clasped while I closed my eyes and concentrated. But almost immediately, I opened them and looked at her, frowning.

'There is someone here, very urgent, very close. But it's not Jamie, it's a girl. A young woman, slender, long fair hair. I can't give you her name, I'm often not good with names. Do you recognize her?'

Janette nodded, seemingly reluctant.

'I think it must be—Laura. She—she died with him. There were three of them, the two boys and—Laura. They all died.'

'She wants to tell you something, desperately,' I said. 'She has been waiting until she could get through to you—you were guided to me, to a medium, so that she could pass her message on.'

'Jamie?' Janette asked, in a whisper.

'Jamie is all right. They are all all right, and Laura wants to tell you that they know now, themselves, that the accident had to happen, this is how it had to be. But Jamie—'

Janette had begun to cry, still gripping my hands as the tears ran down her face.

'Tell him I miss him so much. I can't sleep, I wish I was dead with him, I wish I had been killed too.'

I gave her a little shake.

'Janette, you have to be really brave, you have to face this thing and live through it. Not for your own sake, but for Jamie's. This is what Laura is telling me to tell you. They are all all

22

right, they are ready to pass on the way they must go, the way their souls have to progress. They have let go the threads of their lives here, and they are ready to develop in the place where they are now. But——.' And I faced her squarely, prompted by the need of the spirit of Jamie, which I could feel pressuring me through Laura with greater desperation than Janette's human grief.

'You are hurting Jamie by holding him back. Your sorrow and grief will not let him pass peacefully. You must let him go.'

'I can't let him go,' she wept passionately. 'I love him. With all my heart and soul. Isn't it right to cry for him? Isn't it right to mourn because he's gone, and I'll never—see him—again?'

*   *   *

In the rest of the time we sat together, I did my best to comfort Janette and assure her that her grief was natural and normal, and that the process of mourning had to be passed through after any bereavement. Indeed, was necessary in order to survive the strain that death and loss place on the living.

But I emphasized that she could not cling blindly to Jamie for ever. She had to face up to the fact that he was gone, and let him go, let him pass on his way in peace and free him of the obligation of her terrible grief. Together we prayed, both for the strength and consolation that time would hopefully bring to her, and for Jamie's soul, setting out on its new and fateful passage. Janette was able to look at her loss with courage, to say goodbye to all three of her friends, and to leave me with her grief recognizable as still there, but something accepted, something that would always be part of her. Prompted by Laura's message, she had made her emotional break with Jamie, and would now be able to pass through the process of mourning, and in due course rebuild her life.

*   *   *

Being a medium, and being able to communicate with the dead is basically little different to being able to communicate with the living. Anyone can speak via a telephone to a loved one on the other side of the world, and think nothing of it. A medium simply has an extra sense that enables him or her to mentally 'dial' a number obtainable to others, and contact spirits who are no longer on this physical plane.

Contrary to what many people imagine, the dead are not harmed by contact, and neither are the seekers, though I personally will not undertake to make contact unless the person wishing it has what I consider to be a good reason. My own experience as a medium has indicated overwhelmingly that the dead will answer if they are called, and will respond to genuine need from their loved ones, but I have found that, contrary to what other mediums may claim, they do not usually want to indulge in gossipy chit chat—or even to prove they have survived their deaths. Some spirits return of their own accord to give encouragement and support to the living—often these may be only distantly related, or not related at all. But when most souls have departed this world, they have no further interest in earthly preoccupations and indeed, why should they? They are proceeding with their own individual spiritual development in the planes beyond the earth where they now exist.

I have found that because of their human loves while on earth, they will generally try to comfort and reassure grieving relatives—though they mostly cannot express their state of release and freedom from the bonds of earth, with its physical grief, suffering and pain.

*　　*　　*

I do not know how other mediums make their personal contact with spirits of the dead. Some claim to do it via spirit guides, of whom they may possess several, often the spirits of Red Indians, Chinese, monks or nuns. Sometimes the guides take the form of historical personages, often famous. I have met mediums who have claimed guides as diverse as Edith Cavell, Florence Nightingale, King Charles I and Queen Elizabeth I. The most well-endowed psychic I have ever encountered in this respect claims to possess thirty-six!

I have no spirit guide as such, though I 'tune in' to a powerful 'energy source', which in the long run is probably the same thing. I work directly, in the manner of Prospero, and by concentrating on the name of the person concerned (or some sort of link with them) and the need of the seeker who has asked to make contact, or wishes it, I summon the spirit from the realm it now inhabits. In other words, I call it back. One of four things generally happens, often immediately or very quickly. 1. The spirit will come in response to my call. 2. Another spirit will come instead, often to speak for it. 3. No spirit comes but I feel I will find it if I try harder. 4. The spirit I am trying to contact, or else a different one, is waiting even before I have tried to call it. In this type of case, as with Laura's plea to Janette, the meeting turns out to have been willed by the spirit rather than the sitter, and often involves some urgent message. Or else some message which may, or may not be urgent—one never knows, and just has to give it.

Sandra's case was a spectacular example of this. I had just finished doing a reading for her sister, and they changed seats on the other side of the table, so that I could reach

Sandra's hands.

Immediately I began to open my mind to her (before, we thought, beginning a tarot reading) I picked up a loud, strong presence, and told her I had someone with a message for her. What was more, the message seemed to be about danger, accident, even death. 'BEWARE', I translated, in capital letters. 'BEWARE OF THE TRAINS'. The picture that flashed in fifty-foot neon across my mind was of steam trains, doom, gloom, unqualified disaster.

'It seems to be telling you not to travel by train, particularly steam train,' I said.

'I never travel by train,' Sandra told me, bewildered.

I described the person who was so anxious to pass the message on as a girl of about thirteen or fourteen called Isabelle.

'She was a childhood friend, I think. Someone you played with when you were young.'

After further deliberation, they told me that the only Isabelle they could think of was the sister of a friend from years back, who had indeed lived in the same street, but whom they had hardly known.

'She had red hair, didn't she?' I confirmed.

'Yes, she did.' They nodded after a moment.

'Well, she died young, in about her late teens. And now she is here, warning you about something. But—she was a very emotional, hysterical sort of person, wasn't she?' I asked.

They agreed that so far as they could remember, that had been true. I tried to tone the exaggerated forebodings down so that the message would come across more correctly and interpreted it as a simple warning for Sandra to take care when travelling in general, particularly when tackling steps or stairs. Once I had sorted the real meaning out, I felt reassured that I had managed true communication with the strange, sulky personality who, from the distant past of Sandra's childhood, had been chosen, or asked, to deliver a warning for her future safety.

I deduced that she had performed her errand under some sort of pressure because, once the 'errand' was safely done and I had the message correctly, I 'saw' Isabelle flounce round in her exaggerated adolescent manner, pouting rudely at me as she demanded, as clearly as though I could hear her with my physical ears, 'Can I go now?'

*   *   *

Another unlikely messenger made her presence felt when I was doing a clairvoyant reading for a young man, Luis, at his home. I had been talking about his business, of worries and problems which he kept to himself rather than tell even his girl-friend Donna, who was listening with interest.

I detected several spirits round Luis, and one of them, a man in motor-cycling gear, whose face was covered by his helmet, was apparently well known to him. He had been told of his presence many times, and was as aware of him as of an old friend. But then I began to pick up a woman, and when I began to describe her— colour of hair and so on—Luis declared emphatically that it meant nothing to him. Every detail I added provoked meaning glances between the two of them, but the assurance that they did not know who she was.

'She is getting more definite, but—she seems to be on a seashore. There are rocks, cliffs, and it's dark. It's night,' I said. I was becoming intrigued. 'She is—well, I don't know how this can be, but she is in a *box*. Are you sure it means nothing to you? The spirits are never wrong. My interpretation might be incorrect, but what they give is always, always right.'

Luis looked at Donna.

'It was a cousin,' Donna said quietly. 'One of Luis's cousins. We don't like to talk about it. It was very bad, very tragic.'

'She died—but I am still getting a box, and a dark seashore.'

'She was thrown into the sea, in a box,' Luis said curtly, and I did not feel I could probe this private tragedy further, except that I knew now that the box had come ashore on a sandy strip, with rocky cliffs. Luis nodded his agreement, making no comment. I did not ask why or how

29

the young woman had died, it was enough that it had been tragically cruel and sad.

'She seems to be unfolding herself out of the box, and she has a message, she wants you to listen. She is holding her hands out as though pleading with you to believe her. You must take care in your business dealings, she says. You are dealing with dangerous people. Do not be tempted to go the wrong way, or you will lose everything.'

Luis was listening with head bent, his dark eyes frowning, his arms folded across his chest. I had already picked up a dark side—or more accurately, a potential dark side, the possibility he might be tempted into ways which would do him harm—before the young woman made her appearance, and I had mentioned it. He was not a believer in psychic powers, and this was why, afterwards, I felt that instead of the biker in his black leather gear giving the message, the spirits had chosen a lost cousin he did not even like to think about, one whose end was mysterious and tragic, to warn him of his own possible dangers—and perhaps, by influencing his forthcoming decisions and behaviour, to save his life.

There was no way I could have invented the circumstances surrounding this person, and even if I had been picking up from my sitter's mind telepathically—psychics often do this without even realizing it—she, and the circumstances of her death, were among the last things he would have been thinking of, as even when she made her appearance, he would not, for some time, discuss her.

*   *   *

When I contact a spirit, I 'see' it, as with most psychic visions, via patterns in my mind, rather like arrangements of atoms or electrons. This is also how I 'hear' messages or send them. Apart from certain occasions when the actual words seem to be so close to me physically that I feel as though I am actually hearing them, or the echo of them—Isabelle, for instance, asking sullenly: 'Can I go now?'—everything has to be 'translated' to be comprehensible.

Generally I can tell what sort of words the spirit would have used, and sometimes whole phrases come through, or words I need to 'translate' carefully to make sure the sense is exactly what was intended. I have even, on a few rare occasions, 'translated' from 'cat' or 'horse' when a much loved pet has been allowed to make contact.

This does not happen often—not in my experience anyway—and many authorities do not believe that animals have individual souls. It seems to be considered that all the lesser creatures become at death, part of a huge corporate soul—the soul of dragonfly, for instance, or the soul of zebra. All I can say, however, is that I have been the channel for several individual messages from pets to those who loved them in life.

On one memorable occasion I met my former husband for lunch in a cafe. As we spoke, I picked up that his much-loved cat 'Ash' who had died in tragic circumstances two years before, was being allowed an 'open channel' to make personal contact.

Animals do not, so far as I know, usually communicate verbally, since their minds think 'animal' and this means little to a human being, but Ash had been so dearly loved and his loss had been felt so deeply that an exception was made on this occasion. The little cat sent some simple message that he was happy and comfortable, sent a great deal of love, and tried to blot out visions of his physical death with a sunny, uplifting picture of his spirit at play in a grassy field near a pool, with flowers. Spirits often bring symbolic flowers to bridge the gulf between physical and spiritual worlds, and Ash ended by bringing a large, cheerful yellow sunflower.

On another occasion, I was speaking to a member of a Middle Eastern noble house who lived in London. I had never met his family, and knew nothing about them except that they appeared to live in some rather remote area. I had passed on clairvoyantly a message from his father, and then, suddenly I felt some other presence come into my mind.

'Do you have a horse?'

'Certainly I have a horse,' he said.

'A mare? A beautiful mare? Silver, I think, a sort of silver-grey.'

'My horse is a stallion,' he replied, frowning.

I persisted. 'But you did have a mare, and she was beautiful, a beautiful creature.' For a few moments, he stared at me, then he said: 'Yes, I did.'

'I have her here, she—well, she wants me to—'. I could not find the words.

'Remember her to me?' he said, smiling, and I nodded.

'Yes, that's it exactly. She wants to be remembered to you.'

He did not seem to find this in the least odd, and neither did I. A beautiful horse has a very special relationship with her master in a country where life, traditionally, may hang on the strength of that relationship and though this lovely mare could not form words, she had still managed to send a personal message to the master she had loved.

*　　*　　*

I cannot recall a single case where there has been an evil, threatening or otherwise frightening or upsetting reaction when I have opened contact with the spirit world. This might be so if it was attempted in an atmosphere of fear or negativity, but the spirits who have returned in response to my call—or indeed, turned up uninvited with messages of their own—have in most cases provided intense comfort and hope, as well as their own particular brand of love.

One lady, Maud, looked every inch the 'county' type in her brogues and tweeds. She sat down, very 'laid back' and in control, and told me, with no sign of self-pity, that she had lost her husband a year before, and tomorrow was the first anniversary of his death, and she did not think she could stand it.

When I made contact with her husband, at her request I described him standing on a flight of steps, near a big french window, his face lifted to the wind in a large tree.

'That's the garden—my garden,' she said.

He gave the message that he had never left her, he was all around her, always on the steps and walking in the garden every evening as he had always done, walking with the dog.

'There is a dog?'

'Oh, yes, and we both go to John's grave together, every few days.'

Immediately, I picked up a path overgrown, a lonely place with the grave at the end of it somewhere where the trees opened up to the light.

Her husband was present around her very strongly, and he had a further message, which I translated for her.

'Tomorrow evening, he wants you to set out some glasses—two—and a bottle of wine. And carnations—he said you will know why carnations.'

'They were his favourite flower,' she said. 'The house is full of them. But the wine—who is it for?'

'He wants you to put on his favourite dress—the cobweb dress, he says—'. She coloured, suddenly looking very young. 'Please put it on tomorrow night, and sit at the table—and have the dog with you. Put your husband's carnations nearby, and light some candles. And pour out two glasses of wine, one for you and one for him. This is a celebration, he says, he wants you all three to share it.'

'You mean he will really—?'

'No, he will not be able to drink the wine, and you will not be able to see him. But you will feel him with you, and he wants you both to drink to this particular anniversary, a celebration of all that you have meant to each other. He is around you all the time, you know, he has never left.'

*   *   *

The great love that can exist between human spirits appears to be what provides the main motivation for the dead to return, though it is true that sometimes some can just remain 'tied' to the material plane and enjoy being able to carry on, as it were, as if they were still on earth. One jolly spirit who came back unexpectedly

35

while I was doing a reading for his niece, and whom she identified as her Uncle Alf, could not have been more 'full of life'. He cracked jokes, and generally seemed to be having a great time as the centre of attention. His niece, rather despairingly, said that he had always gone on in that way, but whispered to me:

'How can he! He's only been dead two weeks, and he isn't even buried yet.'

At which point I picked up Uncle Alf declaring with jovial enthusiasm that he fully intended to attend his own funeral, and was really looking forward to it.

'He says he'll be sitting with you in the funeral car and he wouldn't miss it for the world. He can't wait,' I told my sitter, and she could not help a genuine laugh.

'This is mad—but I bet he'll be there, too, and what's more he'll turn the whole thing into a carnival. But at least it's better than crying, isn't it?'

Uncle Alf was enjoying himself so much that it was difficult to persuade him to leave and return—as all spirits must—to his own realm. Eventually, I managed to send him, still wise-cracking and full of beans, on his way.

*　　*　　*

Some of the most unexpected spirits which are drawn by love to return, are those which have never really lived on the earth at all. The bond between mother and child can be wonderfully powerful and overcome all the barriers between life and death. But on many occasions, I have experienced the spirits of children returning to give support and comfort to their mother—only to find that the mothers concerned had in fact had the children aborted.

'I have felt so guilty since,' one sitter, Mary, confessed, overcome. 'I wanted to ask the child to forgive me.'

'There was no need. You were very young, very frightened,' I said. 'It had to be. But the child is here—he—or it, rather, it's in a silver spirit body which has no sex—is here, about so high, (about three feet) with pale silver hair, and it has come to take care of you. Even though it was never born alive, it still accepted the "life" waiting for it and chose you for its mother. And it comes to you now with love. You need someone strong to help you just at the moment, and your child is stronger than you are, so it is here and wants to stay with you—if you will let it.'

The usual response in cases like Mary's is great joy, comfort and reassurance, as well as a lifting of old pain and guilt.

*   *   *

Often there seems to be no rational logic to the way the spirits work—and yet it makes a strange sense of its own. I was talking on the

37

telephone to Andrea, a lady in her sixties who was unhappily trapped in a long-since loveless marriage. Suddenly I told her:

'There is a spirit with you which seems to have come a long way—made a great effort, almost half-way across the world, it seems, to get to you. He has been coming for years, but the time was not right then—now it is. A man—tall, slim, fair, wearing casual clothes, a jumper and slacks, very striking.'

Her breath came quickly. I did not have to ask whether she recognized him.

'I—did not know whether he was dead.'

'He is. And he's come from somewhere like—like the Mediterranean coast—Egypt? Morocco?'

'He spent most of his later life in Africa. He went out there to work after we—parted. It was very long ago,' she said. 'I knew him from when I was twelve, and I—well, I used to write to him when he was away during the war years in the forties—he was older than me. I was in love with him—a sort of mad, passionate romance—though nothing physical ever happened. And then he—he asked me to marry him, when I was nineteen, and I couldn't believe it. It was like a fairy-tale come true.'

'What happened?' I asked.

'I panicked, I suppose. I was terribly young still, terribly gauche. I couldn't face the realities I would have had to cope with, and the—the physical side. Somehow I—let him go, and he went to Africa alone, and I never saw him again. So many times I've regretted that.' She was crying. 'So many times.'

'He is here with you now,' I said. 'And as I say, he's made a very great effort to get to you, he was such a long distance away.' I had a picture in my mind of her sitting alone in her room with the receiver in her hand. 'He's very close, I can see him standing at the door, hesitating, wondering if you want him to come in.'

'Oh, I do, I do. Please tell him to come in,' she wept.

'He's with you.' I saw him putting his hands on her shoulders, and leaning over to kiss her forehead.

The sweetheart of forty years ago had brought his worn, tired darling the message I translated for her as: 'I want to give you the love and support I was not able to give you then.'

I saw him place a strand of yellow beads— amber—over her head, round her neck, and gently kiss her again. 'These are the golden days we were not able to share. Take them now.'

As he stood in the doorway to leave her, he said simply: 'I loved you very much.'

Andrea was more fortunate than most, as she was able to keep her experience with her. Although the necklace of 'golden days' had been only a symbolic vision, I advised her to

39

wear a real necklace of amber round her neck, a physical representation of the spiritual gift of love that she would be able to touch and know to be real. Amber has properties of joy, positivity and upliftment. She did this and wore it afterwards 'from him', finding that she was immensely comforted in a time of darkness, loneliness and need.

*　　*　　*

On the occasions where spirits have not turned up in response to my call, I have sometimes gone to find them. One gentleman was recovering in what appeared to be a camp hospital unit in the desert, of the World War II Red Cross type. He was lying on a folding camp bed, but once I had made contact, explaining my sitter urgently needed to consult him, he conducted me (mentally, of course) to his former home and, wandering up and down the stairs and in and out of the rooms, held a long conversation with me.

It is widely believed that soldiers or others who meet a violent death—from a bomb or land mine, for example—need a recuperative period once they have passed before they can progress further. I did not agree with this theory myself until I came up against several instances like the one above where the spirits were weak and did indeed seem to be resting. But in the cases of which I have personal knowledge, such spirits have not passed violently, but have suffered long debilitation, sometimes mentally, sometimes physically, and often from a long-drawn-out illness.

*   *   *

When people want to contact the dead for reassurance or comfort, prompted by love, I regard this as valid. If the motives are greed (where did he bury the diamonds/hide the map/put the money), selfishness or a demand for proof that death is not the end, in the form of coded questions to which 'only I will know the answer/or the secret word' I find enquirers may receive messages but these will not be what they wanted or expected—though they may well be applicable and very true.

Sharon came to me in great distress, wanting her mother to help her and advise her with her problems. The spirit of her mother came through and made several sensible suggestions, each time being met with a flood of reasons why Sharon was unable to cope and therefore could not follow this advice. Then, after some time, I sensed the spirit losing patience. 'Your mother is saying you have got to face up and not expect other people to run your life for you. She says she can't help, she has her own way to go, and you must learn to do it yourself. I think people have said this to you before, haven't they?'

41

'Yes,' she moaned. 'All the time.'

'Well, it's true—tough I know, but until you can feel you are in charge of your own life, you will never pull yourself out of the mud, and your mother would not be helping you if she smothered you with cotton wool.'

When her mother had gone, we were able to talk about ways in which Sharon could strengthen herself and begin to take control of her present and future. The spirits had given her an unexpected jolt, a dash with cold water, but they were right. Toughness was exactly what she needed, and a push to get her on her own feet.

*   *   *

Another young woman wanted to contact her mother. I picked up a spirit, described her and told the girl she could speak to it and it would answer.

'How do I know this is really my mother?' she asked suspiciously. There was no 'coded word' and the spirit had come through as it had been much earlier in life, as a young girl of about seventeen, round about the years of the fifties.

'I have described her. Do you recognize her?' I asked.

'Yes,' she said.

'Well,' I told her. 'If you recognize the person I have described as your mother, I should think that is proof enough. I didn't know her. There can never be real proof in concrete terms, no matter what anyone says, and the spirits are not taking part in some sort of game. This is a serious business. It is a long way for them to come, often, and involves a great effort. I have called your mother on your behalf and she has come. If you find this difficult to believe and have no faith, you had no right to consult me in the first place.'

The young woman decided—I was sorry to hear—that she was too confused to proceed, and I let the young spirit return to the light. As the sitter left, she looked troubled and drawn—a far cry from the brightness, joy, comfort and peace that afterwards illumines most of the seekers who come with love, trust and faith to speak to their lost ones. A negative attitude, suspicion, demands for proof in case they are being 'conned', might be all very well in psychic investigators or observers who are asking for nothing, but a sitting with a medium is an experience which can be so highly charged that it can change the sitter's life. I have seen this happen many times. Sitters must be willing to 'open up' to the light in the same way I have to open up to it myself—in utter faith and trust.

CHAPTER THREE

CONTACT WITH PAST LIVES

'What is the year?' asked the quiet voice of Oliver, from beside where I lay with my eyes shut on a flat couch.

I looked with my mind and found the figures marked on a long wall.

'Thirteen something—thirteen forty-six, I think.'

'And where are you?'

This was one of my own regression sessions, when I was taken back to my own past existences. It proved traumatic for as the visions came into my head, I began to gasp and cry. I knew intuitively that I was a girl in my early teens, wearing some sort of skin or sacking, and caught up in a vortex of screams, panic, turmoil.

'Fire—there is fire everywhere—it's dark but the roofs are burning, the huts are on fire.'

I could hear myself gasping and screaming.

Oliver's voice prompted me. 'What has happened?'

'It was the soldiers—they came—they're everywhere,' I sobbed incoherently. The tears were streaming down my face and I was shaking violently. 'And one of them, he was a pig, a filthy pig, he—' I could not frame the

44

words. 'I will never forgive him, I will kill him. I swear I will kill him. Pig—filthy swine—I will kill—kill.'

'What else do you see?'

'Everything is red, red and black. The people are running, all directions, there is fire everywhere.'

*　　*　　*

Much of the work I do is concerned with 'regression' or going back to investigate the past lives of my sitters. Examining the lives we may have lived in the past is not just an interesting exercise, being inquisitive or looking for novelty and amusement. In the same way as our childhood forms the adult we become, what happened to us in our past lives sheds light on the people we are now. The lives that emerge for my sitters when I do past life sittings illustrate the difficulties and triumphs with which that particular person is still coping.

Every spirit is here to learn, and the patterns of past lives reveal the lessons that are still being learned today, whether we choose to use this information or ignore it.

*　　*　　*

One past life sitting I did for Tonya, a girl of exceptional gifts and abilities, aged fourteen, revealed two unusual and interesting lives. Both had been men who were 'freaks' and who highlighted their deformities to underline their power. The most recent 'life' was some time in the early nineteenth century, and I thought at first that the creature had not been human at all, since 'it' lived and moved in water, sliding fish-like from surface to surface. It had fish-like webbing between arms and body, and between the legs, and had no body hair at all. I might have placed it in some prehistoric time, but as I examined the 'life' it became clear that this was a man, that he was born a 'freak' and that he had spent his life in some sort of fair or sideshow, and had in fact gained great power by using his repulsiveness to shock and stun those around him. He had also, rather surprisingly, been able to dominate and seduce women.

The second of Tonya's lives took place in medieval France, and this was a man born with no legs, whose arms and upper body became phenomenally strong. He had lived on the streets and terrorized whole areas in spite of his disability. He too had been able to dominate women but through fear.

I told Tonya that she possessed the male strength ('Yang') and the ruthlessness and cruelty of man in a state of survival. But these were enclosed now in a delicate feminine body and she found it hard to cope with them.

The lesson she needed to learn in her present

life was how to 'let go' of power and domination, the manipulation at which she had been so successful in the past, and also to accept just being ordinarily human, not to flaunt her eccentricities and her differences to other people—even her gifts. She admitted she did not really relate to other people. I could see that so long as she retained traces of arrogance and used her sense of being different to feel superior, she would find it difficult to be happy.

*   *   *

When we regress to a past life or lives we are given new insight into the patterns of our own personal existence, and into the karmic laws which govern the cosmos—the laws of cause and effect, of wrongs being redressed and efforts and achievements being rewarded, of the components of balance. The problems or struggles we may be having in our present life have been reflected or foreshadowed in the past.

Making contact with our past lives can help to clear up loose ends, to redress old wrongs, to find peace of mind and to know and understand ourselves better. Often the revelations of the past are the last thing sitters expect to hear—as in the case of Anne.

*   *   *

Anne came to me for a sitting in some distress.

She explained that though her family roots were in a small village in Norfolk, she herself had never visited the place. Until recently, when she had decided to buy a country cottage there.

'I fell in love with it—the church, the little rows of cottages,' she told me. 'But it was incredible. I can understand a sort of feeling of familiarity with the village itself, from hearing family memories, but I am getting more than that—I go for walks and come to places I seem to know—know well—including the inside of buildings, and yet I have never been there in my life. What do you think is causing it? Am I just seeing a sort of *déjà vu*? Or is it something deeper? I feel as though these places mean something to me, but how can they?'

We sat down and began the session. I held her hands and concentrated, waiting to see what would come through.

'I'm seeing a woman, fair, very fair, slim and young. I think you lived in this place before. Can you ride?'

She looked bewildered. 'No.'

'You could then. I can see you riding out, set against the dawn, misty in the autumn, coming from some trees, by a gate and across furrows, wide fields, to meet a man. He's waiting. His name was James, and your name—I think it was Anne in those days, too.'

Her voice was breathless with excitement.

'I know the place you mean, I saw it and

48

recognized it when I was there, I knew it meant something. And James—'

'Was he a relation?'

'The only James was the name of my great-grandfather.'

'There's a lot of passion here. What was your great-grandmother's name?'

She thought for a moment then said: 'Emily.'

'What I am seeing doesn't seem to make sense, then,' I said. 'In your other life, you loved this man, and he loved you. It was like something in a dream, something too wonderful to exist. I can feel his surge of passionate longing, his love. You were his wife—for a time, and then you died young, about twenty-four, of consumption. But if you were Emily, you were your own great-grandmother.'

She stared at me with wide eyes, suddenly excited.

'My—my great-grandfather was married twice. His first wife, so far as I remember, just trying to think of the family history, died very young. Her name might have been Anne—I'll have to check. She had no children, the line went on through the second wife.'

'It was the first, the one who died. She looked like you, too,' I said. 'Have you a picture?'

'I'm not sure—there might be one, an old Victorian picture, you know. Somewhere. But

49

I'm sure you're right. I feel as though I remember James.'

'I think you have felt a great sense of loss in this life,' I said, and she nodded. 'Something you can't identify, the loss of someone very dear to you.' Again she nodded. 'But you have not lost anyone who should matter to that degree. So you have been mourning inside, without knowing who you were mourning for, or what.'

'Yes,' she said. 'You are right. I could never explain this to anyone, but that's exactly what it has been like.'

'You were married to James,' I told her. 'You were his first wife, you lived in that area.' I described the cottage which had been her home.

'I saw it, as it had been inside, and I knew I'd been there,' she agreed.

'Your marriage was based on a deep love. When you died, James was devastated. He married again but he never forgot you. You used to be with him in the dawns, when he went across the fields to work, in a silvery mist; he would see you waiting by the dark trees. And you would wait for him, unable to be parted from him.'

She had begun to cry softly.

'I miss him so, it's as though my heart has been ripped out. Even after all this time.'

'Time is relative,' I said. 'He still longs for you, in the after-world where he is now, and you, in your new incarnation, long for him. Even though he was your great-grandfather, he was also your passionate lover and husband.'

Linking in with the 'Anne' she had been, I was able to unite the lovers across the time and space that divided them, so that each was free to remember their love and accept that of the other. Anne was able to feel she had found the missing part of herself, and I told her that the spirit of James too now felt they would never be parted. But at the same time, having been united, they were able to let go in faith and trust that their love was stronger than death.

Anne was much comforted as she left, and I told her to go to the places she had recognized and she would find James was there in spirit. 'There is nothing to fear,' I said. 'Your relationship is something precious and beautiful—and it will not get in the way of a real romance for you in this life. Think of it as a story you read once, a love story that will stay with you and bring you inspiration and joy.'

*   *   *

Mara was another sitter who found an unexpected dimension in her past life sitting. She was slim and attractive, with thick masses of blonde curls and a piquant face. She was bright, pretty, seemingly cheerfully optimistic and obviously the mainstay of her family. But

51

she admitted that she was not happy, and was toying with the idea of leaving her husband and teenage sons. I held her hands and concentrated to link in with her past lives. The image that came to my mind, which I described to her, was of a swine-herder in some country that seemed to be part of medieval Europe, though it was impossible to be sure. The person in this past life had been accustomed from a very early age to live in a remote area away from other people, with only the pigs for company. She wore rags that were filthy and stained, and were hardly ever replaced or washed. Her hair was matted, and every so often was hacked off with a knife. She had hardly any sense of language, merely grunts, and no vision at all of civilized living. She ate her food as the pigs did. I assumed she had been female, though she herself seemed unaware of any difference between the sexes, and the nearest she ever got to finding warmth and love was when she lay down to sleep with the pigs.

At first, Mara could not identify with this poor creature and the poverty of her existence, but when I pointed out that she had been complaining bitterly about the way her family treated her, making her home filthy and leaving their possessions everywhere in an untidy mess for her to put to rights, never considering her needs or wants, she got the point.

'I'm living with the pigs all over again, sort of, aren't I? It's true—and I get no love, or thanks.'

'I feel that the woman who cared for the pigs felt close to them in some way—one of them almost,' I said. 'She seems to have been very fatalistic about her life, but it was very limited—she knew of no other. You can see alternatives, and it's the conflict which is upsetting you. Starting again on your own will be a big step, and you've been used to the status quo for a long time now. People find it difficult to change even if that change is for the better. But basically, it's quite simple. Do you want to look after the pigs for the rest of this life, as well as in the past, or do you want to strike out for an independence where you're not a slave who gets nothing except the task of cleaning up the muck?'

Mara found the prospect of breaking with her life of drudgery too much to cope with, though she said she would think about it. But I suspected that she would probably stay with her husband and family—even though she felt cheated, demeaned and bitterly miserable. In the same way as the swine-herder had identified with her pigs and found her own comfort in their company, Mara too preferred—for the moment—to keep to 'the devil you know' rather than the frightening prospect of being on her own.

There are different ways of exploring past lives. It is most usually done by means of a light hypnotic trance, or sometimes by relaxation, without the subject needing to go into trance. As with the psychological experience of 'abreaction', which returns to a trauma or incident in early life, the subject can experience his or her past life for himself, and will react to it. Such regressions need to be handled with care, as they may be painful or emotionally upsetting.

I use my own method where the sitter does not need to regress, and which can be undertaken anywhere, usually sitting across a table, holding hands. When I concentrate, I empty my mind of images and ideas. I do not ask the sitter whether they have previous knowledge of a past life, as this would be a suggestion. I sense the power in my mind combing space and time, and, as though spotlighted, one figure, or one scene or image becomes more and more clear.

Variations in the 'lives' which have revealed themselves have been staggering. Investigators in this field have tried to identify past lives recalled by subjects, and to prove their veracity by 'dating' them and relating them to recorded history, but most of the 'lives' I have linked in with for my sitters have been impossible to check, sometimes even impossible to relate to this particular planet.

One young woman, for instance, had lived in some unspecified time that was obviously prehistory, in a place where the whole sky was blood red. I had the impression that the sun was still burning so fiercely that if she had been on the earth, it had not yet cooled to the world we know. What was more, she and all the other inhabitants of the place had been timid, four-footed creatures, who were vegetarian and nibbled delicately at tufts of what seemed to be moss or grass, with no inclination to attack each other.

Most of the people who lived in the past were ordinary and unspectacular, uneducated and unremarkable. The mortality rate was high, armies came and went, women were lucky to survive childbirth. It does not surprise me that many past lives I have encountered have been of infants or children who died young, and that I often 'pick up' on the life at the point of death.

One of the first past life sessions I can recall doing was with a young woman called Alison.

'You were with pioneers in the New World. Not fighting the native Indians, but defending yourselves against some other group I can't identify, though I sense lawlessness and violence, since they all had guns. You were very young, a little girl, about four. All I am getting is that you and your people were in some sort of cabin or building, firing through the windows—or slits, or whatever. I can't see them because you were crawling on the floor, trying to hide, and all you could see was the boots, big boots and people's legs, wearing dark clothing. And the fire. You crawled to the fire for comfort, and I can hear it crackling and see the glow. And then the door crashed open and—they, whoever they were—came in.'

I paused.

'What happened then?' she asked.

'It was quick. In the chaos, one of them got hold of your ankles and swung you hard against the wall, smashing your head in. That's all there is. You went. You were gone.'

*   *   *

Not long after I began working with past lives, I wrote: 'I have known what it felt like to be in the arena in Rome in the moments before the lions attacked. I have crawled, covered with boils and unable to walk because of malnutrition and rickets, among rotting cabbage stalks, trying to eat them because there was no other food. I have stood, a black girl slave whose tongue had been cut out, waving a tall fan throughout the long days in ancient Egypt.'

I have also encountered more active participants in their ongoing development as a soul. Catherine sat down with me at a psychic fair to try and contact the spirit of her father, who had been estranged from her, and when I described the spirit which had arrived, she was puzzled.

'None of that is a bit like my father.'

In fact, the gentleman had been her father in a previous life in the late Victorian era. He had been big and bluff, a self-made man from the dock area of London, with interests in shipping. He lost his wife in childbirth, and had been left with a delicate little daughter, whom he worshipped. Catherine had been that daughter and she had died from tuberculosis in her early teens, leaving her father desolate. So, feeling her call to 'my father', he had arrived at the psychic fair to give her, if she would accept it, the love, support and encouragement he had been unable to bestow on his frail little girl, taken from him before her time.

Many sitters feel they can identify people from their past lives in their current situation, or recognize them when they appear, but Catherine was unimpressed by the sudden visitation of a doting father. She did not dispute his existence, but she said she could not remember him and he was a stranger. She was not at all sure she wanted him in her life—even though she had been telling me previously how empty of parental love that life seemed. By the time she left, they had formed an uneasy truce—and I thought that perhaps Catherine's case was a good example of 'not getting what you think you want, because you won't know what to do with it if you get it.'

The case of Rick illustrates how past life sessions work. At each sitting, I make notes so that the sitter can take away a report with a description of the lives that have been revealed, and how I have applied them to the present. Rick sat for a past life reading on 26 July 1994, at another psychic fair I attended.

He was a rather bohemian young man who appeared to be in his late twenties. I asked him nothing about his current life, and set to work to make a link with the past. The notes I wrote for the first life I contacted were as follows:

'A boy about eight years old in a hut in some Scandinavian country approx 1500. Outside is snow and dark, of which he is (atavistically) afraid. Inside the hut is warmth from a round stove, light, happy voices talking, father (?) making boots out of skins. He clings to the warmth.'

Rick identified immediately with this, and said he understood the two realities I sensed in the boy, the clinging to a known security and the fear of the dark unknown. It reflected his own attitude to his current life, an inclination to dwell in the past and an apprehension of what the future might hold. He also identified with the Scandinavian link, and said that in the distant past there were family forebears from that part of the world.

He said he felt close to the boy, who had not

lived for much longer. I picked up a death a few years later by accident in the snow. Rick seemed morbidly preoccupied with death, and this did not surprise me, for while linking in to the boy, I had also seen a sweeping panoramic vision of hundreds, perhaps thousands of previous lives where he had been children of both sexes who had not survived childhood. In all these cases they had been sacrificed as part of the culture in which they lived—I particularly glimpsed ancient Chinese and Japanese civilizations, where deformity and slaughter had been considered a mark of honour and importance.

I noted down: 'Plus—Chinese and Japanese and other cultures—children of both sexes being ritually murdered or deformed in sacrifice to "deities", treated as objects, given futilely—many, many early deaths.'

Yet another life developed this theme even more. This time I saw one more child, a girl of about eight in some early civilization that seemed 'in a hot, sunny climate', who had lived apart, marked for sacrifice since her birth. I saw her being taken to the place of sacrifice, and described what she was wearing—a garland of flowers round her head, and a sort of skirt that seemed to be made of thin strips of wood and stuck out from the waist to about knee length at an angle of some 45 degrees, like the top of an umbrella or the shape of a wide bell. She wore nothing else apart from ritual items of flowers, and I wrote:

'She is not afraid but she does not have any idea what this is about.'

Rick felt that the picture which was building up shed a good deal of light on his feelings in the present. I told him he was just beginning to learn to leave a symbolic clinging to the irresponsibilities and fears of childhood behind and move into acceptance of an adult life. At first he had not feared, even when there was danger, but now he was fearing when there was no real danger. I felt he was carrying the many deaths he had endured, often vainly, and his past sacrifices were a heavy load.

At the end of the notes, I wrote a summary of what we had discussed during the session:

'You have been hurt and murdered futilely many times over. At first you accepted this without fear and with no comprehension. Later, when you learned to be afraid you became terrified of phantoms and clung to the warmth and security of childhood. There is a split in your character—you must learn to look forward to living, not to anticipate or desire the escape of early death. Accept the future and let the past go.'

*   *   *

When undertaking a past life session, one never knows what will emerge and the way in which I work is a protection for my sitters, who would probably not be able to cope with the full force of a past life of horror if they regressed to it themselves.

I was doing a sitting for Doreen, and we had seen two comparatively pleasant lives, when the third came, like a vicious and unexpected blow. As I linked in with it—a young woman in medieval Italy, who had lived a sheltered life and married a neighbouring landowner, during a happy and innocent wedding celebration—the cold and the dark of what had come to her after the wedding was so strong that I needed to make a conscious effort to fight off the power of the negativity and was left shaking with reaction.

I told her what I had picked up. She had married a sadist who had taken her to her new home, kept her a virtual prisoner, beaten her, and in particular subjected her to terrifying sexual abuse. She had conceived several children and lost them because of miscarriages induced by her husband's treatment. I felt 'much pain, many dark threads of reaction to the pain and to the evil itself.' She had married at about nineteen, and was dead by the age of twenty-seven, completely broken in body and mind.

Significantly, Doreen did not want to identify with this life, though my feeling was that she would come to recognize similar sufferings and abuse from some of her other past lives when she was more able to face them and began to have confidence that she could cope with them.

*　　*　　*

Such terrible past lives can do damage if they 'hit' a sitter who is unsuspecting, and it is not necessary for sitters to experience the lives themselves to be able to react to them and benefit from them. The only real way a life can be 'proved' to be authentic is in the effect it has on the person to whom it is linked. If the sitter responds with a sense of rightness, of recognition, as though he is connected with a missing part of himself (or, sometimes, a part of himself he does not want to acknowledge) a genuine connection has been made.

There can never be proof of past lives which would stand up in court. Once again, the sitter needs faith and trust, the psychic needs complete integrity and a willingness to open up to the spirits and what they choose to give. Occasionally, though, something happens to verify my vision of a past life. In the case of Maeve, I told her I was picking up a middle-aged woman in France at the time of Joan of Arc, a 'pillar of the community she served', a respectable and respected midwife with a grown-up son of whom she was very proud. But this lady was not all she seemed, and when Maeve told me that another psychic had told her previously that she 'was a prostitute in

Paris' at that time, I was able to explain that she had indeed been a very young and very unsophisticated prostitute, come to Paris from the country when she was in her late teens. She had had a child, learned to toughen up and find ways to survive, and I had picked her up not as the young prostitute but as the respectable middle-aged matron who kept her past to herself and had carved out a new life of respectability for herself and her son.

Often on other occasions I have picked up past lives which were not quite as subtle as Maeve's, a peasant woman or slave perhaps, and the sitter has told me afterwards that he or she had been told the same thing by other psychics.

I have never (to date) picked up any past life for a sitter which was recognizable as a well-known historical personage, though this is probably only a matter of time, since sooner or later such people are bound by the law of averages to emerge. Perhaps the most unusual cases I have experienced were past lives as animals. One lady sitter had lived in about AD 500 in the Russian steppes as a young bear, which I saw being hunted and tortured by riders on horseback, a dark and brief life in a dark landscape.

The other was during my own regression session. After several lives—the raped peasant girl of the fourteenth century in the burning village; a Civil War gentleman—I went back to find I was a thin, stray ginger cat, wandering round the boots of the habitués in a public house in London at the beginning of the 1800s. I was hungry, I had no home, but I was at peace with the world and with myself. I was content to live for and enjoy the moment and to let tomorrow look after itself, trusting in a greater power to provide what was needed.

I have always believed in the traditional ancient wisdom of cats—after that regression session I was more than ever convinced that true learning does not necessarily come out of books!

CHAPTER FOUR

LOST, HAUNTED, POSSESSED

The first case of the sensational, darker side of psychic work which I encountered was very near to home—the subject was a colleague in his fifties with whom I had worked closely for several years. But the incident came at a time when I was not in charge of the situation myself and therefore was not able to deal with it in the way I would have preferred; but this first-hand experience helped to confirm my theories on 'possession' and haunting and taught me a great deal.

The popular picture of 'possession' or

'haunting' involving the unquiet dead, dark deeds recurring, manic and criminal behaviour, helpless individuals being used by overpowering forces against their will, is one which, by and large, does not exist. I have dealt with many instances of 'haunted' or 'possessed' personalities, but they do not evolve in the ways commonly imagined, and they do not behave in the ways the uninitiated believe. Neither does one deal with them by dramatic gestures such as exorcism—which in fact is extremely negative, since it casts the unquiet spirit into outer darkness and denies it the right to salvation—or pointed stakes, silver bullets or other trappings of sensational fiction.

Any type of haunting or possession, however it comes about, and even if the haunter or possessor is a saint, Christ himself or the Buddha, is unnatural and therefore needs to be resolved if at all possible. The unfortunate people who find themselves suffering the stigmata of Christ are affected just as negatively as if they were being 'possessed' by the devil. For the body and mind each spirit is given to inhabit during its life is its own, and is not there to be 'sub-let' to other entities. So anything within us which is not of us is an intruder, however much we may cling to it or wish it could remain. In order for each spirit to proceed, any haunters or possessors have to be dislodged and helped on their rightful way—and that is where the psychic comes in.

The most sensational case of 'possession' I have witnessed took place when some ten people were gathered to sit in an Open Circle. The most senior member, May, who usually conducted the proceedings, was not present, and her 'deputy', Kevin, was in charge. Before we began, he scrupulously took the right precautions to ensure that we were protected and no negative or evil influences could penetrate the circle, and we started working on meditation and visualisation. It was about twenty minutes later when, very quietly and unexpectedly, one of the members I knew, a man in his fifties called Charlie, began to show signs of distress.

At first, he claimed he was unable to unclasp his hands, which were locked tightly together. Then he tried to speak but seemed to find it increasingly difficult to communicate. He was still sitting, as we all were, but within a few seconds, Kevin was on his feet, commanding him urgently: 'Charlie, come back, come back. Charlie, you are to come safely back here with us, now.'

Other, more senior members of the circle joined in, to give their assistance. Several took up dramatic poses of the 'warding off evil' type, on different sides of Charlie, who was now complaining something about 'them' who were standing beside him and seemingly trying

66

to 'take him with them'.

I stood quietly apart and watched. In a case like this, it can be dangerous to touch the person involved, in the same way as it can be dangerous to startle or touch a medium in trance, as the shock to the system when the soul is absent from the body can be so great it might even kill. In any case, I was not in charge and there was nothing I could do without interfering with what was already taking place—there was plenty enough of that. Kevin had Charlie carefully by the arms and was urging him to his feet, walking him up and down as one might walk a sufferer from drug overdose, to keep him aware and stop him drifting into coma. It was evident that Kevin thought Charlie's spirit might drift into some other dimension if it was not sternly recalled.

The rest of the circle, apart from the group which was attempting positive activity around Charlie, held their places. They had no idea what to do, and some of them said afterwards that they went icy cold so that they almost collapsed, but though they were very frightened, they bravely clung on, feeling it would help to hold the circle together. Something was obviously very seriously wrong.

Kevin turned to me.

'They, he's saying. "They". Who does he mean? Do you know?'

I replied reluctantly.

'I think so. He worked with a well known rock group in the Sixties, and he was very close to the leader, Steve. He's talked quite a lot about him recently, wanting to contact him—and another member of the group, Johnny. They both committed suicide—I know Steve hanged himself.'

By now, Charlie was being assisted to shuffle up and down but complaining his feet were not touching the floor and that there was something round his throat stopping him from speaking. The word 'hanged' hovered ominously in the air.

'Is it Steve and Johnny?' shouted Kevin.

Charlie mumbled 'Yes.'

'Why are they here? Did you ask them to come?'

Charlie did not seem to know, but horror shook the helpers.

'You don't want them here, send them away,' Kevin ordered.

'Can't. They're—my friends.'

The tension was mounting, then to top everything, the door opened and in came May, the group leader. It was as though the Archangel Michael had decided to intervene personally. A sob of relief went up from those clinging to the circle. She stared at the incredible sight, Charlie being frog-marched up and down while magical passes and protective signs were being made on all sides of him. A few words filled her in, and she leaped

68

into the fray, joining Kevin.

'They are not your friends, Charlie, they are your enemies. Tell them to go.'

Charlie almost sobbed, torn. 'No—friends.'

'They're trying to hurt you—kill you.' May was adamant.

'Charlie, come back,' Kevin ordered, eyeing Charlie's face. 'Tell me your name. Who are you?'

'Who are you?' May repeated.

He did not seem to know.

'Tell them to go, and tell me your name,' Kevin yelled.

The noise was overpowering, shrieks, shouts, other members calling 'Charlie' and 'Come back'. The whole incident carried on in this way for some twenty-five minutes, until at last, Charlie seemed to calm somewhat, was able to let go his hands, seemed to recover his senses and sat down, in contact with the floor again. The fit of 'possession' had passed.

In the anticlimactic atmosphere that followed, people muttered to each other that they had not realised at the time just what was happening, it had all been so quick, but now they could see that—well it had been a close shave. Kevin and May later informed me they thought that Charlie had brought the attack on himself by inviting the spirits of the dead musicians to return. The evening was obviously over; subdued, everyone went home.

That was the end of the incident, except that

the following evening, at half past twelve midnight, I had a phone call from Charlie, who told me 'something' was with him again in his bedroom, and he did not know what to do. I talked to him for an hour until he felt calmer, helping him mentally to rid his room of negative influences, using visualisation and light, sending energy so that by the time the hour was up I was so exhausted I was in a state of collapse. There were no more visitations, but by then I was more convinced than ever of what had really happened at the 'possession'.

Had it been the sad ghosts of Steve and Johnny recreating their suicide and trying to take Charlie's spirit with them beyond the grave? Or an evil spirit which had broken into the circle? It was a fact that one of the sitters that evening had been a stranger nobody knew, but who had struck everybody (so they said afterwards) as being in some way 'weird' and 'menacing' right from the start.

My own personal conviction is that there were no spirits present, whether of Steve, Johnny or anyone else. The whole thing was, in my view, nothing but an attack of hysteria, and if Charlie had been properly dealt with it could have been controlled within five minutes. I suspected even while the incident was occurring that May and Kevin had no real idea of how to cope with 'possession', whether genuine or not, and were greatly disturbed by what was taking place, but as I have explained,

I was unable to interfere. Instead of trying to concentrate on the positive aspect, and helping Charlie and any wandering spirits towards the light, to calm and peace, the issue had been confused with insistence on 'enemies' and danger and 'telling them to go away'. The incident turned into sheer melodrama, feeding on itself, and all that was missing was a gigantic gold cross conveniently to hand to be snatched up and held, Van Helsing-wise, before Charlie's face.

Fortunately, Charlie was unaffected and no serious damage was done on that occasion, but this case illustrates in the clearest way what most cases of so-called haunting and possession are based on—hysteria, imbalance, ignorance, suggestion, fear.

*   *   *

There are, however, genuine cases where the body—or more usually, the mind—is invaded to some degree. More often than not, they are accidental rather than deliberate, and hardly ever involve full-blown activity on the part of the devil or the forces of evil. There are many times where it is difficult to differentiate between so-called mental illness and types of possession, and in questionable cases, I personally always refer the patient to skilled medical help. Often the application of healing and 'just being there' can help, but as I have

71

said, I never try to solve everything myself, and psychics are not the only people who have their part to play.

Some cases involve possession which attaches itself to its host for no apparent reason. One black man, Aaron, sat down with me for a reading admitting he was afraid.

'Things just happen round me,' he said. 'Somebody does something I don't like—upsets me—and the next thing I know, they've fallen off the roof, or crashed their car, in hospital. Nothing I do, but it happens.'

I was able to pick up that from some far-off ancestry, some distant heritage, he was carrying with him a primitive type of voodoo power—but pre-voodoo itself, and also with its roots in Africa not in the Caribbean. This was a very savage, evil concentration of energy which had chosen him for its host, and of which he himself was personally and thankfully free. He was acting as a channel for it to expand its own powers, but in reality, it had nothing to do with his own personality or his own thoughts, wants, or personal feelings.

As in all cases where entities are concerned, spirits need to be sent on their way, but there was no spirit here as such, only the force, and I recommended first of all that he protect himself and work at consciously developing his own spiritual strength. Awareness of the force would certainly help, and I also suggested that he brought in some 'big guns', as it were, by taking the force to places where it would feel undermined and outclassed. Negative powers cannot flourish when they are swamped by positivity, and if it felt the strength of stronger faith and belief, it would probably remove itself to find a more congenial home. His fear, too, was feeding it at the moment.

He admitted he was not particularly religious, but I told him to visit churches or meeting-places of every religion or denomination he could think of, and allow their strength and influence to sweep through him and fortify his own positivity.

Concentrating hard, I prayed with him, summoned down spiritual power and protection and called on my own energy sources to loosen the hold the thing had upon him and free him. He seemed incredibly relieved, and went off to buy himself a crucifix and a necklet with the name of Allah on it—a double guarantee of protection—from the jeweller across the street. I felt certain that the renewal of hope and the awareness of the fact that, though he was not to blame for the disasters that were happening around him, there actually was a real problem to be solved and some positive action he could take, would give him enough energy to free himself of the negative power around him.

Many cases of possession by spirits, demons, djinns and such creatures as incubi and succubi can be compounded of frustration and desire, expression of fears or wants, craving for power and attention and an excess of mental or sexual energy which may prove destructive, if not actually evil. I came across one lady—of Eastern extraction—who claimed she was possessed by a djinn which was always with her, would not leave her alone and kept her very active sexually. I was unable to get rid of the djinn—largely because, although she complained about it, she would not allow me to make a serious effort to try. Also, I deduced clairvoyantly that she relished the sexual power and the reputation as a worker of 'black magic' that she enjoyed, and she had no real desire to be free of these expressions of the darker side of her nature.

*　　　*　　　*

Genuine cases of possession or of lost spirits or hauntings seem to arrive unexpectedly and often without the victims being aware of them. But when they do make their appearance, it is impossible to mistake them. Usually, I pick up right at the beginning of the session—even if the sitter has come to me for a tarot reading or some other reason—that there is something that needs to be dealt with, and generally it is obvious that some sort of possession is involved, though the exact details may need working on.

Lynn came to me in the setting of a psychic

fair held one evening in a room behind an Irish pub. The atmosphere was cheerful and friendly, she looked normal enough as she sat down across the table—poised and confident, an attractive woman in her twenties. But as soon as I took her hands, I could feel the presence of the cold that signifies contact with spirit activity and in this case, with tragedy and suffering, pain and death.

'Were you abused, starved, beaten and shut up in the dark as a child?' I asked and she shook her head in bewilderment.

'No, of course you weren't, not in this life. But in a past life, you were. In a past life you lived such a terrible existence that when you died, the little spirit was not even aware it was dead. It has stayed with you—it is still with you, and is around you all the time. It is not aware it has been reborn into another body, it thinks it is still existing in the hell of that terrible life.'

I asked whether she was aware of the situation, whether she had been told by other psychics of what had happened. She was very thoughtful as she replied:

'No, but in many ways it doesn't surprise me. I have been told often that people can sense a child with me, even though I have never had a child or even wanted one particularly. And though my own childhood was happy, and I loved my parents, I have always had a feeling I couldn't explain that I was carrying some awful dark burden and sort of—of—.'

I waited as she struggled to find the right words.

'Well, like crying inside, bleeding in my heart if you know what I mean.'

The child in her past life had existed, I told her, in the last century, probably in some big city like London, though it was difficult to be sure, as it had spent its whole life confined within one room which I thought was a sort of attic, high up in a building I could not identify. It had never learned to walk, never learned to talk, never known the companionship of other people. It had received no love or affection. The room where it lay—its bones stunted—was never cleaned or aired nor the filth removed. Every so often—I could not judge the time—the door would open and the figure of a man would appear—though the child was not able to recognize it as a man, in the same way as it was unaware of its own self, so that I was not able to identify whether it had been a boy or a girl.

I could not tell what relation the man had to the child, except to feel his animal brutality, (true possession if you like). When he came in, he would fling a few scraps of food at it, lash it unmercifully with a rope or a belt, then leave it, bleeding and hardly conscious, without a word. This was all the life the child had ever known.

Lynn was holding on to my hands as the

picture unfolded. 'He—or she—lasted about six years,' I told her. 'Then it—you—went.'

'What happened?' she asked steadily. So far as I could tell, nothing had happened except that the man had simply not come. The door remained closed. I thought the man had died elsewhere by violence, and since no one else was aware of the existence of the child, it too died, from starvation, and the awful remains in that ghastly room mouldered and rotted unrecognizably in an eternity of sad decay.

'It is still going on,' I told Lynn. 'The child did not pass from the dark to the light as it should, so time has stopped for it, and you carry that room and what is in it with you. We have to release you from the possession, or the haunting or whatever you want to call it, otherwise you won't be able to progress and grow in this lifetime, as yourself. Does this make sense to you?'

She nodded slowly. 'I know it's fantastic, but it seems as if this is something I've always known, deep down, but without knowing what it was, if you know what I mean.'

'Do you feel you want me to go ahead?'

'What do you need to do? Exorcise the child?'

'Send it to the light, release it and help you to let it go,' I explained. 'It's in the wrong place. It must be given rest. But it may be traumatic for you—after all, it was just as much a part of you as you are yourself in this present life.'

'No, no,' she insisted. 'I want it to be released and laid to rest. I can feel that's the right thing to do.'

With the cheerful sounds of the psychic fair all around us, we continued to hold hands across the table, and I shut my eyes and set to work. I asked Lynn to repeat the Lord's Prayer quietly with me, and prayed to the source of light to take the small spirit of the child into its keeping and give it rest. I drew on my energy sources to break the eternal hell of the moment in which the little spirit was existing, and bring it peace. I felt the battered and tormented little soul pass across its barriers and helped to ease it gently on its way, trusting the light to provide for it.

I asked Lynn to concentrate on the child which had been her former self, to visualize it leaving the dark of the attic, of going from her across a great green meadow towards the distant hills beyond.

'Let it go,' I instructed her. 'Say goodbye, wave to it, see it on its way. Help it to go home.'

Her eyes were tightly shut, tears were slowly trickling down her cheeks, her hands clutched mine. She moved her lips in a prayer, then opened her eyes and gave me a crooked little smile.

'It's gone, I can feel it. It's gone home.'

'Now we must finish the task,' I said briskly, aware that she needed emotional release—but not ready yet to let her cry.

Together, at my instructions, we returned mentally to the dark attic and I cleansed it spiritually with prayer and light and power. We lit every corner, swept away the filth, the memories of pain and despair. Mentally, I guided her to place armfuls of fragrant flowers, to set white candles and light them so that there was sweetness and love to replace the dark and the suffering.

'You may need to mourn for the child,' I told her. 'You may feel deep emotion, even as though you have lost a child of your own. Remember, it was you, yourself. So let yourself mourn if you have to, and be aware that you're helping the little spirit to pass. Light candles for it when you get home, put flowers for it, say prayers in some place you think is special or holy, give it the love and remembrance it did not get when it was alive. You will find your own personal peace as well as giving the child peace.'

She nodded, close to tears, but with an expression in her eyes that told me she was able to look forward now, and would no longer be drawn back to the dark.

There was one last ritual. Together, we returned for the last time to the empty attic, where flowers and candles filled the space with peace. I had had an impression that there had been little light able to penetrate the room over the years, so I flung wide the windows and let in air, the breath of life, and the gold and blue of a sunny sky. The dark place within Lynn's soul, which she had carried with her for so long, was cleansed and purged at last. We smiled at each other across the table as she dabbed at her eyes and I began to bring the sitting to a close. Just one more visitor at the psychic fair, which was still in full swing—but within the last half-hour we two had been far beyond the barriers of life and death.

*　　*　　*

So what exactly is the nature of the sort of evil that is encountered in possession or haunting? In Lynn's case, as we can see, there was no intention to do harm—apart from the cruelty of the man who had abused the child in the past—and he was probably no more than a callous and brutal example of an often brutal generation, not some sort of limb of Satan. Lynn even told me afterwards that she could identify very strongly with the man as well as the child, and asked: 'Could it be possible that he's reincarnated too? That he might be in this life with me?'

I told her it was very likely, that the participants in this sort of situation—or even the people closest to us who we love in families or groups of friends—come back together, over and over, perhaps in different relationships, maybe in masculine rather than feminine guise. I have already mentioned the need to play out our cause and effect debts under the karmic and cosmic laws that govern the universe, to pay for the bad we have done and be rewarded for the good, and I explained this to Lynn.

She seemed to understand. 'I think I know who he is. And he is still harming me, in a way. He'll have to pay for what he did to the child, won't he, either in this life or another?'

'Yes,' I said. 'But the child accepted an incredible load of suffering, and has gone right up on the credit side, karmically. Maybe the wisdom and spiritual progress you gained through your suffering in that attic will let you understand him now. I don't think he's very happy, is he?'

She smiled. 'No. And maybe it was intended that I should be strong enough to help him ... forgive him.'

'You do feel you can forgive him?'

'Yes, I do. Now that the child has been put to rest and all the dark is gone. It just doesn't seem worth being vengeful and bitter. It's now and the present that matters, isn't it?'

*   *   *

It is this sort of positivity and spiritual growth which marks all dealings with cases of possession. Even when one is dealing with seemingly random evil, such as poltergeists, the investigator generally finds that the 'poltergeist' itself does not exist as such, but has been created from negative energy, usually emanating from a disturbed personality that is in need of help. Almost all the evil one is likely to encounter as a psychic turns out to be the expression of weakness, fear, or the need for help.

Through facing the fears and weakness, accepting the need to go forward and grow, we can free ourselves of the clinging ghosts of the past, the demons of pride and jealousy, envy and hate.

Often it is not easy. Carol came to me at another psychic fair, held in a very elegant and sophisticated hotel. She looked young with her natural blonde hair and soft skin, and when I took her hands I picked up a 'secondary personality' around her, which I thought was from a past life, one which had not left her. Again it seemed the personality of a child, though in fact she was in her thirties with two children.

It was difficult at first to identify the child 'possessing' her. I tried several past life regressions but the first two were sketchy. The first was a small girl who had apparently survived a ship-wreck with other people in unidentifiable seas, some centuries ago, and whom I picked up in distressed circumstances clinging to a sort of raft in heavy seas. I did not think the child had lasted much longer—and she also seemed to have been deaf and dumb, or retarded.

The second life was even more sketchy. An infant, a toddler, perhaps two or three, I could not tell the sex, which had never learned to talk, living on a Polynesian type of island which was destroyed by an erupting volcano, when the child died along with every one else.

But by now Carol was beginning to find the situation made sense. Neither of these children could speak, and she told me that she suffered very much, and had done all her life, from being unable to express herself—as though something was stopping her from saying what she wanted to say. I had also picked up the child presence clairvoyantly, and felt that she was unable to grow, to be an adult.

The third life brought the answer. She came through clearly, a little Puritan girl in a dark dress and white cap, who had gone with her family to the New World. She too had died young—and she had been dumb. I felt that it was she who had been 'haunting' Carol, even that she had probably accompanied her into her other, more recent lives.

'If we leave her, she will continue to hold you back, and transmit her fear—because she is very afraid. Do you want me to send her to the peace where she belongs?' I asked. 'The decision is yours.'

Carol said she supposed she did, and we proceeded to lay the little girl to rest in the same way as with Lynn's child. I told Carol to think of the little girl, to visualize saying goodbye to her, to watch her walking away across the green meadow—at which point Carol broke down.

'It's all right, she is safe, she's gone home,' I assured her. 'Now you are free to be yourself, to be able to speak, to say what you want to say, to grow.'

But Carol, who had previously declared she did not really care about the child going to rest, seemed far more affected than had Lynn. She said she felt bitterly bereft, as though she had lost a large part of herself, and she wished the child had not left her. It was obvious that she had been far more 'possessed', to the exclusion of her own self, than Lynn had.

It takes courage to face up to 'possession' and to come through it safely, which is why I always explain the situation and let the sitters decide whether they really want the situation changed. Often there is sadness, mourning, adjustment, and always, the growing process which brings wisdom and new confidence and strength. All those who ask for help will get it, but there is a right time and right place for everything, even dealing with each individual 'possession'.

*　　　*　　　*

One venue where I have attended psychic fairs seems to me to be 'haunted', in a very sad way.

84

The hall is behind a pub. And seems to me to have been built on a site where old drovers' roads might have ended and herds of animals been penned together before being sold or even slaughtered. The hall is always cold, and I pick up an atmosphere of the animals' panic and fear, something sad and pitiful. In some cases, such an atmosphere can play itself over and over like a record stuck in a groove. Happy atmospheres too can work this way and make some places joyful. In the chilly hall where the ghosts of the little creatures mill helplessly round together, I have burned brown and green candles—the colour of the earth to which animals are so close—to lay their fear to rest and prayed for them.

At another similar venue—the function room in a pub, complete with elaborate draperies and lush carpets and soft lighting—I encountered a haunting that even I did not recognise at the time. I went into the room in high spirits, prepared for a pleasant evening, but within half an hour I was suicidally depressed. My family had all gone, I was alone in the world, and I was becoming increasingly sure my partner did not love me—didn't even care—wouldn't care if I died. There was no hope. No future. Nothing. I sat in a corner and refused to speak to anyone, withdrawn completely into myself.

It was not until, with a tearful struggle, I managed to pull myself away from the experience, away from the place and the evening, that I recollected that the pub was haunted and had recently been the scene of two exorcisms by psychics I knew well. The disturbing presences had been sent on their way, the spirits laid to rest. But after that evening, I felt certain that, so far as I was concerned, the negative presences were just as powerful as ever.

A ghost will often be something unexpected—a feeling, a mood. And negativity always goes to the weakest spot, the weakest link in the chain. In my case, my greatest fear is of rejection and abandonment—it had hit the target in the centre of the gold. And what was even more intriguing was that I had not, throughout the whole difficult, painful and upsetting evening, connected my mood with a 'ghostly presence'—not even though I knew at least one man had committed suicide in that building and was known to haunt it.

The sadness which can linger on is something to deal with compassionately rather than with fear, if one can. I feel the despair of mind that drove that particular suicide to his death, the disquiet of the frightened animals, is just as important as the case of the young man who sat down at a fair in Torquay and said bluntly to me:

'I think I am possessed by the devil.'

When I asked why, he seemed at a loss.

'Well—I don't know.'

When we reached the root of the problem, it turned out that he had no confidence and had been having difficulty getting a job. He was also experiencing trouble with his girlfriend. And his parents. It all boiled down to the normal traumas of adolescence, in which the devil did not seem to be even remotely involved. He left much comforted by the reassurance that he was no better and no worse off than everyone else. But I felt his novel approach to the problem did indicate a refreshing originality of thought.

CHAPTER FIVE

SEEING CLEAR

It is not always easy to differentiate between the various sorts of 'sight' I possess. I was born with so-called 'second sight', which is really no more or less than the power of clairvoyance—though over the centuries second sight has been taken to mean an ability to foretell death.

This is true to some extent. A psychic can often tell whether a sick person will die or will survive, or can 'see' death around a sitter, and generally when it will happen, though I personally find I see far more often their tangled destinies in living. But death can make itself apparent, usually in an unexpected way.

I was attending a venue one afternoon—'on call' as it were—when a man presented himself suddenly and asked whether I could do a reading for him the next day, as he had no time just then. He was perhaps forty, with an engaging smile, but he looked strained and worried.

'I hope you can fit me in,' he said. 'I have a lot of things I want to sort out, and I've been to two other clairvoyants but they both refused to give me a reading.'

'Why was that?' I asked.

He shrugged. 'I don't know. They said they couldn't get anything and there was nothing there.'

'Well, I will do my best. I'm sure we can find something for you,' I assured him, and he arranged the booking and left.

As he went, I picked up some sort of attack that left me weak from hyperventilation and negativity. It was difficult to fight it off—and I knew then that he would not come back the next day. He was about to die, suddenly and probably within hours, of a heart attack. There was nothing anyone could have done, and the violence of what had hit me needed about ten minutes to control and subside. He did not return.

*   *   *

Another time I was doing a clairvoyant reading

for Clanna, a tanned young woman brimming with health and enthusiasm for life. She was working in a hotel temporarily but wanted something more out of life, and I was able to link her with activity in a distant, war-torn African state, where she would be accompanying some sort of film unit, either making news footage or a documentary film.

She had asked me about relationships in the future, and I told her:

'Because of the danger and the nature of what you are doing, you will be very close to the people you work with, even the men. But as close friends who might save your life rather than anything else. They will seem closer to you than your own family—you'll have gone through so much with them, they'll seem like extensions of yourself.'

'I like the idea of that,' she nodded. 'But—what about love?'

'Oh, you won't have time for love affairs and neither will anyone else, you'll be far too preoccupied—too tired, in too many tight spots.'

'Sounds exciting,' she smiled. 'But—will I have a love affair later, then? And get married?'

As I looked into the future, I saw it was blank. She would die aged 32, shot during the fighting while crossing some sort of a bridge made from creepers under fire. She would never have a lover.

I looked into her bright face and said:

'I think you should wait until your job's over first, and then see what's in store for you. Things seem a bit taken up with your adventures just at the moment.'

For all psychics are aware that nothing, even the fate we can see so clearly ahead, is sure. The future consists of layers of alternatives, alternative realities which depend on the teeming small decisions we make every second, and how we cope with what comes our way. And there are always miracles.

*   *   *

Seeing things which are 'not there' can take various forms. Sometimes the things may not appear at first to make sense, but it is vital when working clairvoyantly to give the sitter *exactly* what you see than try to make sense of it yourself. The psychic must pass on the message exactly as it is given—it is for the sitter to find the sense in it, and you may find something that seems irrelevant to you has vital meaning to them. In one case I was doing a reading for a young woman and I received a vision of a railway crossing.

'Does this mean anything to you?' I asked my sitter and she nodded without explaining further.

'And I have,' I began doubtfully. 'I don't see how this can be right, but I have a large red and green parrot.'

'My boyfriend,' she said briskly. 'He works on the railways, and it's his parrot.'

'He wants to tell you something, communicate with you,' I told her.

'But I'll see him in two days. Is it something urgent? Should I phone?' (She was on holiday on the other side of the country.)

'No, no,' I said. 'When you see him will be fine. But he has something to say to you which is important.'

I did not think we would ever meet again, but some months later, she happened to be in London and contacted me. She had been impressed with what I had told her, and revealed:

'When I saw my boyfriend, I just said to him, what is this special thing you want to tell me, then?'

'And he was staggered. He did have something to say to me, something very personal, and he'd been wanting to say it for some time, but afraid to, wondering how I would react. My asking, just like that, made it easy for him, but we were both amazed at how I had known.'

*   *   *

Clairvoyance can help to clarify things, give answers, rather like having an 'answering-service' to set the mind at rest over problems and queries. This is where the 'clear seeing' comes in, and the cases where sitters have had

91

their worries sorted out—whether they choose to accept the answers or not—are so numerous, and often, so seemingly trivial, except to themselves, that it would be impossible to list them. Several versions of the type of situation given below happen almost every day:

* * *

Maggie, seventeen with soft brown hair. I hold her hands to link up.

'You're very stressed. I think you are afraid. Can you tell me why?'

A quick, nervous smile. 'Oh, nothing, really. It's just that—well, I'm starting a new job next week and ...' she hesitates.

'Yes, I know. You worry a lot, don't you?'

She nods gratefully. 'It's a smart office, and I didn't think I would get it.'

'I have a feeling you've never got much encouragement at home. You've been criticized a lot. Do you have a brother who gets more attention?'

She seems grateful again for the insight.

'Well, yes, but he's good-looking and he's studying to be a doctor and ...'

I spend the sitting working on Maggie's confidence, looking into the future and revealing to her that if she sets her mind to it, she will not only do well in this new job but will have the chance to employ her good brain and powers of organization, her cool headedness and ability to take responsibility, in much higher posts. She will be a powerful lady—and, what is more, her foundation of integrity and personal morality will bring her happiness. She is also—and I tell her this—aware of her abilities and of what she can do, given the chance. She has simply been conditioned over the years to doubt herself.

'You can do it,' I tell her. 'You are like a flower just about to unfold—you just need that bit of sun to help you see who you are and what your potential is. Don't be afraid—go in there next week and knock them for six.'

Glowing, smiling, confident, she reaches out impulsively as though to a dear friend and gives me a hug.

'Call me when you're Boss Lady and you can treat me to a lunch,' I tease.

'I will,' she grins, and turns to go, bright and radiant and seven feet high.

*   *   *

Moira told me of the difficulties she was having with the woman she worked with, how cold and unfriendly this woman was and how unbearable it made her job. I picked up the woman, whose name was Carmen, and realized that she was behaving in such a cold and unfriendly way because she was acutely shy and did not want people to realize her vulnerability.

I suggested to Moira that the next time they

spoke, rather than exchange the barest minimum 'hello' or 'yes' and 'no', she should make a comment on Carmen's name and ask whether she was fond of the opera which was her namesake. 'Don't worry,' I advised Moira. 'She will not snub you, I can guarantee.' Often the advice given by the spirits via clairvoyance, or the answers which come through 'seeing clear' require a good deal of personal courage, and I imagine that many sitters are not able to take this sort of step. If they can, they make great strides forward in their spiritual and personal development. Even something as simple as risking a snub from a person who already seems threatening does not come easy, but I heard later that Moira had taken my advice, and the two women had talked enthusiastically about Bizet's *Carmen* for half an hour, all the barriers broken down. Moira could not believe how seemingly miraculously her inaccessible workmate had turned into another human being.

*   *   *

Ellen is a sophisticated lady with a brittle beauty that comes from expensive treatments in beauty salons. She takes my hands and immediately I say:

'You have given up. You feel nothing any more, do you?'

'You could put it like that,' she says.

'Your husband. He has been your whole life, and the children. But you have had enough.'

She gives a little sigh and says simply, 'Yes.'

'I don't think there has been any problem with other women—or men—has there? I am picking up your husband and I see that through the years that you have been married, you have continued to grow—but he has not.'

'Yes.'

'In fact, you feel no love for him any more, but you are sorry for him. Your pity is very strong. You know how weak he is. That's the cause of the trouble. You simply want to continue living and growing on your own— with the children—but you can't leave him because he wouldn't be able to let you go, and you are so sorry for his inadequacy.'

She says nothing, but the compliance is there.

'He comes across as a very strong man in his public image, very successful in his professional life,' I say, and she gives a wintry little smile.

'Oh yes, very.'

'Good-looking—magnetic, I'd say— charming. He can convince people he is larger than life. But you know that inside, he's like a little boy.'

She nods again. 'Absolutely, that's absolutely it.'

We try to sort out the options. Ellen has no axe to grind, she simply wants to be free to continue her life in her own way—leave the marriage peacefully. I feel her need very strongly, as though she will die from the claustrophobia of her life unless she is let loose. But at the same time I sense too the fatally binding link of dependence and pity which holds her to her successful, charming husband. I see she will not be able to leave him without a great deal of soul searching and personal effort.

One of the precepts I continually pass on to sitters as a psychic is that no one can carry the karmic burden of another soul. We are each responsible for our own lives and for what we do, but we cannot and should not try to be responsible for the lives of others. Ellen is carrying her husband's karma of weakness and clinging dependency, which sucks, vampire-like, from others. Often love is the excuse given for such behaviour, but real love gives without asking for reward or measuring what has been given. We outline and explore the possibilities and actions Ellen can take, but as she leaves, my feeling is that she is not ready yet to let her husband go and I think she will carry on as usual. I discover privately later that she has been coming to clairvoyants for years in the same state, asking for advice on the same question.

*   *   *

Often clairvoyance helps in 'seeing clear' the

realities of situations which are not what they appear on the surface. Lois, in her sixties, tearfully sat down to ask when her lover would leave her. He had taken over her home, drank and spent her money, did exactly as he liked, and gave her very little in the way of affection in return.

'I can't stand it,' she moaned. 'I've asked him to go, and he takes no notice. But it's ruining me. There's someone else I might take up with but how can I with him there, rolling in drunk and whenever it suits him?'

I could see that all she really wanted was a chance to talk about her situation. She would have been lost if the lover had left her, and in fact, when he did some months later, she aged considerably and sat down just as tearfully to recount how she wanted him back. She tried in every way possible to get him to return so that she could keep up her long-standing saga of woe again. But anyone who had taken her situation at its face value—according to her own words—would have assumed she was an unhappy victim of an unscrupulous male.

*   *   *

Clairvoyance can encompass everything from being able to detect worry in a sitter and often to identify what the worry is, to evidence of cruel treatment in the past, to emotional problems, stress and phobias and the many

97

threads that make up the pattern of our human life. It can just as easily pick up shining enthusiasm, nobility of character, a gift for giving, and—when this rather rare element is present—deathless love which will transcend all that heaven and hell can offer. Clairvoyance is in fact the traditional 'sixth sense', being able to use the 'third eye'. A clairvoyant can see things not visible or apparent to other people, it is as simple as that.

*   *   *

Though clairvoyance deals with living, it should not seem frightening that a psychic can see death—after all, we are all, sooner or later, going to die. Death in itself is merely a fact of life. It is the fear of dying which causes the trouble, and this is a necessary part of the human make-up and condition—without this curb we would all be queuing up to jump from the top of the Post Office Tower or the Empire State Building, lemming-like, since this world is far less comfortable than the place we will pass on to.

But possessing clairvoyant power brings a big responsibility, and visions of death, as with losses to come of longed-for children or other catastrophic happenings, have to be dealt with by the psychic as he or she sees fit. I try in circumstances such as these to dwell on the positive aspect without necessarily making promises I know are not likely to be fulfilled. For instance, I have dealt with many cases of women of all ages who have asked eagerly: 'How many children will I have?' or 'Will I have a child soon?' or other similar questions. Often when I look into the future I see the answer is a miscarriage, several miscarriages, difficulty in bearing a child at all, or the baby's death.

I usually advise (as appropriate) seeking medical advice and help, being prepared for minor surgery, concentrating on the live healthy child which will be born later rather than the ones which I can see will be lost first. Also, since the power of clairvoyance is not intended to know all the answers but to help prepare and cope with whatever the heavy load of living may bring, I try to give strength to the sitter to carry whatever losses or disappointments they may have to bear and point out that it is not the events which happen in our lives that matter, it is how we cope with these events and whether we face them with courage and positivity, learning from them and gaining strength, or whether we are negative and allow them to make us bitter and angry. Much of the work of a psychic involves spiritual teaching, and one phrase that comes up time and time again is that: 'We are here to learn and the lessons are often hard; you can let them break you or you can let them refine you like steel in the fire, and grow stronger from them.'

*   *   *

Many sitters who feel they possess psychic powers have 'seen' events which later happened clairvoyantly—rail and plane disasters, natural disasters as well as family deaths seem to be the most common. The disasters do, however, have something to tell us, even though we may not always be able to work out what it is.

Mark, a sophisticated young executive, came to me for a sitting and when I asked him whether he had any problems he wanted me to deal with specifically, he smilingly shook his head. 'Not a thing.'

'You are married. Happily?' I asked.

'Absolutely idyllic. We get along well, we're easy with each other, we allow each other space, there are never any problems at all.'

I felt there was something wrong somewhere but I was unable to put my finger on it. Each had a successful career, there was no jealousy, no competition, no single flaw, it seemed, in this relationship. And Mark shook his head to all my queries of problems at work, family, domestic—everything I could think of. Finally, I asked him, reluctantly:

'Could you imagine marrying again, being happy with someone else?'

He frowned.

'No, everything is so perfect. Why? Is something going to happen to Val?'

I chose my words carefully.

'From what I see, she will not be with you about six months from now. Could there be another man?'

'No way at all. The only thing that would separate us is death,' he said, and asked me straight: 'Is she going to die?'

Following the guidance of the spirits I replied; 'She might well die. Unless you save her.'

He seemed very cool. 'What must I do?'

I described to him the message I had been given. His wife, I said, was in the habit of taking long walks on her own, and he agreed that was so. She did not like fussing or interference, I added, and again he agreed I was right. She would not take kindly to his insistence on her telling him where she was going, I told him, and he nodded.

'That's just like her. Independent.'

I asked whether they lived near a deserted place where there was water and stretches of desolate land—an old quarry, I thought, or moor, heath. He replied that there were several areas like that about.

'Your wife will go for a walk in one of these place and catch her foot, twist her leg or her ankle. She will not be able to walk or to tell anyone where she is. She will probably die from exposure, lying there so many hours. (It was a very cold November). It will be an accident, pure and simple, no violence, nothing. But,' I added, 'you can save her.'

'How?' he asked hoarsely.

'For the next six months—and if they pass without incident, she is safe, the accident will not happen—make sure you know if possible where she goes. Do not be put off by her wanting her privacy and her independence. If she should be missing, do not hesitate longer than a few hours before getting help. She will be in one of these lonely places with a broken ankle or leg, suffering from exposure. But you must not wait—make a scene and even if the first time you find she's perfectly all right and you feel a fool, do it again if it happens a second time.'

He thought for a moment, then said, 'It's up to me then.'

'You can save her,' I assured him. 'If you do not follow these instructions I have given you, she will be dead within six months. By pure accident.' He thought for a few moments more, then nodded. 'Thank you. I'll do it. If I lost her I don't know what I would do. I already suffer from severely high blood pressure caused by stress.'

That was my break-through, in the last minute of his sitting, that my early suspicions had been right and that there was something very wrong indeed with this young man who apparently had everything, and not a single care in the world. I also felt that there had been some underlying message for him about his relationship with his wife which was far too deeply repressed for him to admit to me. The spirits, however, see all, and I felt that this apparently ominous presentiment of the future had in fact been one which would prove positive for both him and his marriage.

*　　*　　*

Another case which involved some sort of warning of doom happened when Joanne and her sister Hazel sat down for a reading, which, as so often in such cases, turned out to be a three-sided discussion rather than a one-to-one. It was a happy affair, and Joanne and Hazel laughed and exchanged mutual glances that said, 'What did I tell you?' as we progressed.

Then I caught a picture that was different.

'Do you ever go to motor-races?' I asked. 'Or does anyone in your family drive a fast car—a sporty type of car?'

'No,' Joanne answered, subdued by the tone of my voice. 'No—'

'What about the bikes?' Hazel suggested, adding to me: 'We all go to the motor-bike rallies—Jo wouldn't miss them.'

'Your children too?'

'Yeah, we go together, like a family outing.'

'I can see that there is going to be some sort

of accident or crash, a bad one. Spectators will be hit. A child may die. It's a little girl, about six, with very blonde hair, long, loose.'

Joanne wasted no time.

'We just won't go to any more,' she said briskly.

'No, I think this knowledge has been given to you so that in some way, you can help to stop the crash happening,' I told her.

'How?' she said blankly.

'Just by being there. By being careful and by urging other people to be careful. It might even be that the racing scene is only a symbol, and the crash might be something as simple as a bicycle accident in the road when you're doing your shopping. Or else, if you come across anything like a petition, or some sort of action which is being taken for safety on the roads or with motor or bike racing, join in. This is a sign for you to play your part in stopping that small girl being hit, stopping the scene I saw with spectators crushed. Just be aware, and by doing that and taking any other action you think will help, you will stop the crash I have just described to you. Even the smallest thing might make all the difference.'

'Do you think so?' she asked wonderingly.

'I know so. I might make mistakes, but the spirits never do. Do your best, be aware, be there. And you will be responsible for saving lives.'

'I'll let you know,' she said, as they left. 'If

it happens.'

It never did. Probably because Joanne had faithfully carried out the instructions she had been given clairvoyantly.

*   *   *

Clairvoyance is not always concerned with the great issues of living, the life and death matters. I was talking to Ishma, who I knew worked in a bank. We dealt with her problems regarding personality clashes, and then I added:

'There is something—a small annoyance or ache—that affects you when you are at work.' Obvious irritations for a bank worker might have been tension in the neck, headache, eye strain, but instead I felt impelled to continue: 'Like a—joint stiffening up, or a—toe hurting.'

She gave me a slow, mischievous smile.

'Well, it is my little toe, actually, it has layers of hard skin and it rubs.'

CHAPTER SIX

ANGELS, ALIENS AND STAR
CHILDREN

Amanda takes my hands and I look at her. There are three questions I need to ask, and I know already what the answers will be.

'You have always felt different to other people, as though you did not belong, haven't you?'

'Yes,' she says eagerly. 'Alone. Isolated. Even though I come from a big family. I just never seemed to fit.' She shrugs in rather an embarrassed way. 'I don't know why.'

I do but I keep it to myself for the moment and turn to question two.

'I think that at some time in your early life, in early childhood maybe, you had the equivalent of what people refer to as a near-death experience. Did you ever go into a coma, or under an anaesthetic for an operation, and you were told later that it was difficult to bring you round?'

She shakes her head doubtfully.

'No—not really.'

I wait, knowing there will be more to come.

'But—I was accidentally buried under a sand fall, on some dunes when I was a baby. I can't remember it, but apparently it took hours for the fire brigade or whoever it was to dig me out, and people said it was a miracle I was still alive.'

I nod. This is only what I have expected. I go on to question three.

'You feel often that you want to go home, I think.' Before I can proceed, her face seems to crumple with pain as though I have touched on a nerve, and she says:

'Yes, yes I do. All the time.'

'But which home do you mean? Where you live now? Where you used to live?'

She shrugs again, without speaking, then says in a low voice: 'I don't know. Nowhere I am aware of. I just—want to go home.'

*　　*　　*

Amanda is a star child. She is not of this world and comes from another plane, though I do not care to be drawn into discussions as to where, exactly, this plane might be. I only know that star children exist, that when they come to me for a sitting, I can usually recognize them, and that if there is any doubt the answer to the three questions I have mentioned above will generally clinch the matter.

Star children are 'visitors', elevated or advanced spirits which have returned voluntarily to take on another human incarnation and help souls which are still learning in some way. They are also learning themselves, perhaps to cope with some defect such as arrogance or pride. They are sometimes aware of their unusual status, but because they manifest singly rather than in groups, they generally keep their feelings to themselves. Many are very unsure of themselves, believing their awareness to be the product of their imagination.

Another star child I encountered was Eric, who sat down without comment and gave me his hands to hold. He was unimposing and anyone passing him in the street would not have given him a second glance.

I looked into his face.

'You know, don't you?'

He nodded, saying nothing but with a little smile.

'You've been alone since birth.'

'I lived in Africa. The animals raised me.'

It was simply said, but whether he meant it symbolically or literally, I knew it was true.

'Your near-death experience?'

'I fell into a pool as a toddler. I was under the water for twenty minutes before my "body" was brought out. I was still breathing.'

I held his hands for a moment without speaking. Often when dealing with such an elevated mind it is possible to communicate telepathically and say a great deal which could not even be said to another psychic. Star children recognize each other, and know each other without need of human explanation and (as one myself) I find encounters like this as uplifting as unexpectedly bumping in to dearly loved members of my own family.

'You have a great destiny in Africa, in one of the states, one of the new kingdoms that keep emerging there,' I said to Eric. 'You know about it, don't you?'

He nodded. 'Oh, yes, I've been preparing all my life. And I have no doubts. The greatest spiritual leader there has already named me his heir.'

I smiled. 'Then why did you need to have a sitting with me? You don't need me. You don't need anybody.'

He smiled back. 'Perhaps as a treat—for myself. Before the hard work starts.'

*   *   *

Claudia had come to me because she wanted a child very badly and she and her husband had tried for some time without success. When she explained the problem to me I saw that what I was about to witness was one of the most touching miracles I would ever see. Claudia, though a sophisticated woman whose clothes bore designer labels and whose long blonde air had been expertly styled, had the sweetness and innocence of a child. She shone in the hotel room where the psychic fair was being held, brighter than the lamps and candles, the crystals and gem-stones that decorated the tables of the psychics.

Claudia believed in miracles. And she was to be granted one.

I told her that she and her husband must go on a 'pilgrimage' in the same sort of way as medieval couples travelled to sacred shrines to pray for a child. There is great psychological validity in this too, since the journey together, the complete break from work, the closeness and dedicated purpose of the trip will often result in a letting go of pressure and tension and under such circumstances conception is more likely.

Claudia asked where they were to go. I was given instructions clairvoyantly that it did not matter except that it had to be as far away as possible within this country, and that it must be some place they both considered 'holy' in their own particular way—since Claudia's husband was not religious and she herself was not quite sure about organized religion. Often in cases like this the ancient affinity with the beauties of nature, water, the sea, trees, mountains and old traditions can work best. I suggested somewhere in the north of Scotland—the Isle of Iona is, according to directions I often receive from the spirits, a particularly hallowed place.

I told Claudia not only that she would conceive, but that the child which would be born would be a star child, who would bring its own special light into her life and the lives of those around it. Only twice (as yet) have I been able to predict the birth of star children, but in Claudia's case it seemed especially fitting that the birth too would have been 'announced' by the spirits.

It was to be a tiny girl on which they bestowed as a second name the one I had given to Claudia—'Joy'.

*   *   *

There are many echoes in the psychic work I do of all the great religions. For instance, I have had cases of angels making their appearance as well as (for want of a better word), 'Messiahs'. My first 'angel' case came as rather a surprise, though a very touching and uplifting one. I had never previously seen anything I could remotely describe as an angel, and I did not expect to see one on this occasion.

Aimee, a long-standing friend whose husband had just died was struggling through the difficult weeks after his death, knowing that her much loved and faithful dog, Donny, was dying too after a long and full life of companionship. I had met Donny over the years, but lived the length of the country away from them both, and when I phoned to ask how he was—how they both were—only to hear her say bravely: 'He came to the end of the road on Monday', I could imagine her distress.

She felt it would be a comfort if I could pick up any message from Donny, and I got him at once, pushing a posy of white flowers, a type of snow flower I had never seen, a plant with silver leaves as well as silver flowers, meant for her, along the ground with his nose. After a few moments of memory flashes, I felt a change and told her: 'He is still himself, but he has connected now with what I can only describe as the great soul of "Dog", the great power and strength that is "Universal Dog", "Eternal Dog". He is very strong, very dignified.'

111

'That makes a lot of sense to me,' she said. 'I know what you mean. He was such a softy, but he was always so strong, such a great spirit.'

'It's as though he has joined with his own kind, and become both himself and something greater than himself. He is fine, but concerned about you. He has come back to be with you—although you know he is there as himself—but he seems to be there in a different sort of way too, sort of growing and spreading as though around you and protecting you—like a—well, like'—there was no other word for it—'an angel.'

'I felt that, I knew what you were going to say,' she whispered, and told me that the thought comforted her a great deal.

I saw no form or face, but tall shapes which might have passed for angel wings, in colours difficult to describe—the nearest I could get was a sort of soft grey-blue mist with silver and cloud and feather deep within. This type of vision—I had seen others though not in such close connection to a departed spirit—probably forms part of an etheric or shamanistic body and I believe that this is how most 'angels' or even 'guardian angels' really come into being.

*　　*　　*

Another case which took me into the realms of the mystic, away from more usual work, also involved an animal and happened when a fellow-psychic, Emma, asked me to try and contact her departed and much-loved cat. I picked up the spirit straight away and told her: 'Linka is a horse now, a lovely and powerful horse pulling a sleigh across great tracts of snow in some place like Russia, she's helping to rescue people I think—save people who are lost in the snow.'

Emma was disturbed at the news. 'She is working. Not at rest.'

'She is saving people, Emma. And she is such a beautiful animal now. Would you have her do anything else? You can be very proud of her.'

She thought about it for a moment, then accepted it. 'She was so good. I got her from the cats' home,' she told me and I said immediately: 'Well, that makes sense. You saved her, and now she is saving others. She is putting back into life in her way the gift of life you gave to her.'

*   *   *

There are many different types of 'aliens' among us, but not of the little bug-like green monster variety. Many times, though, I will take a sitter's hands and say: 'You don't belong here, do you?'

Always they are grateful for the recognition. I have never had a case where the sitter gave me

113

a blank stare and said they had no idea what I was talking about.

Not all are from other planes. They may be from another time or they may be only partly human. When Alicia sat down, tossing back her long, straight brown hair—an ordinarily attractive girl of twenty-two—I looked at her closely.

'You have a power which is not of this world and comes from another time,' I told her. 'Something which you are already aware of, and which will cause tragedy in your life and the lives of other people without your being responsible, and in spite of what you may do to avoid it. I think you know what I am talking about.'

She looked deeply into my eyes and then said simply: 'Yes, I know.'

'You are an enchantress, and it is your fate to inspire deathless passion in men that will drive them mad.'

She bent her head. Her voice was just a whisper. 'I honestly do nothing. Nothing at all.'

'I know,' I said, encouraging her through her hands, which were holding mine surprisingly coolly. 'You just have to be there, that is enough. There have been men already, haven't there?'

'Two—but not—in the way people would think,' she protested. 'I didn't even notice them, and absolutely nothing happened—you

114

know, between us, nothing at all. One was my boss—I don't work for him now—and he was like, my father's age, I never thought anything about him, I wouldn't have been interested.'

'I know. Sex is not involved. This is enchantment,' I agreed, and she went on:

'It just came out of the blue. He wanted to give up his wife, everything, and run away with me. The more I tried to stop him, tell him I didn't want to know, the worse he was.'

'I am afraid that's how enchantment works. The more you "spurn your adorers", to use an old cliché, the more deeply they fall under the spell. What happened in the end?'

She shrugged uncomfortably. 'Oh, I left and when he realized it was no good, he sort of broke up and went round looking like it was the end of the world. His wife took him back, I think, but she'd taken it very badly and his business was affected too.' She paused then added: 'It was even worse with the other man—he kept threatening to commit suicide. I thought he wouldn't but he did try it, in his car with the exhaust. His son found him in time and—well, he's all right now.'

We sat for a few moments in silence before I began to talk to her. I knew there would be other men—far too many men—who would be seized by the same passion for her, the same unaccountable and impossible desire to possess her and 'own' her. She would never be able to have an ordinary love affair of her own.

115

She belonged in the world of elemental spirits, of legend and myth, of fates which hounded men's souls to death but were themselves cold and untouched by human emotion.

The real tragedy, I knew, was that her own emotions were precisely of that same faery coldness, and we talked for a long time about how best she could protect herself and others against the gifts with which she had been so cursed, and try to live as happy a life as possible in a world where she did not belong.

*   *   *

Another case involving an 'elemental' was that of Morgan, who told me with melodramatic pathos the tangled story of the love problems in which she was involved. There was a large cast of characters—her children, safely being taken care of, for she was a good mother—and at least three men in her life: a husband, who for various reasons was unsatisfactory; a lover, and another younger man, all making demands on her; she was torn, she said, abused, she didn't know what to do—but as she spoke, I picked up on her 'elemental' qualities and I challenged her.

'On the one hand, I think there is a point which must be taken into account here, Morgan. You are what is described as "amoral". Be honest, now, I am not judging you, but I feel you have no understanding of

116

what morality is, and you live by your own
"morals"—or in other words, without
conventional morality. This is something, a
quality some people just have—like having
blue eyes. But I think you see no reason to be
faithful to any one man, do you?'

After a moment of weighing me up
measuringly, she dimpled and shook her head.

'Fair enough. But it might well get you into
difficulty because other people will not
understand why you behave as you do.'

As she started to protest about how
unreasonable the men in her life were, I
interrupted her: 'There's another point, too.
You complain about their behaviour, but I
think things are actually the other way round.
If your life was peaceful and orderly, just you
and your partner nodding by the fire, if there
were no complications with men, I think you
would go out straight away and create some.
You complain about being used by these
lovers, but in fact, you use them yourself like
some sort of mischievous sprite, you mix all the
elements up and stir so that you can enjoy the
resulting chaos and tangles. It's you who lead
them a dance, not the other way round. I know
I am right, however much you might deny it.'

She had come to ask me what she should do
to resolve the love problems, but again, after
glancing at me for a long, hard moment, she
dimpled once more, as though she was
acknowledging I had 'seen through' her, and

agreed that very probably, I had the truth. Under these circumstances, I told her, it was almost impossible to deal with her tangled love affairs, as she would be so miserable without them and without assorted men around her that the first thing she would do would be to go and create new tangles and new lovers for herself.

I felt she had the same faery coldness as Alicia and was very much of an elemental spirit, a tree nymph or water sprite. I advised her to at least try to be honest about what she did, and felt. To an outside observer she was very much a victim of the men around her—but, as I had told her, my feeling was that the person pulling the strings of the puppets and enjoying the show was Morgan herself.

*   *   *

The realms of 'aliens', nature spirits and myths can bestow warmth as well as cold, and can bring dreams true in the most fairy-tale manner. The case of Sara wonderfully illustrated this. She came to me in a sad state, eyes dulled, hair lank, miserable and depressed, seemingly with no interest in anything. I told her (though even to me it seemed rather unlikely, but I do not argue with the spirits) that her life was about to change. She was from a different world, I said, she was from the realms of romance and legend, and she was on the point of meeting the knight who would literally sweep her off her feet into a glorious summer of love and sunlight—what was more, he was already in her life, though she did not yet realize his identity. I also worked to give her healing and upliftment, and she left seeming somewhat comforted, though still forlorn.

It was perhaps nine months later when, hearing I would be present at another psychic fair, she came to find me. I did not recognize her—where was the waif in this lovely and shining woman?

She hugged me.

'It all happened exactly as you said—my Sir Lancelot—the summer of languor and love—everything came true.'

I asked her to put down in her own words the story of how the seemingly miraculous fairy-tale had happened—here it is:

After my reading with Dilys, I felt uplifted and so happy that she had picked up that I was out of this world. I had always felt that I didn't belong here and that it was difficult for me to stay here on this planet. However the more in touch with my spirituality I became, the stranger I was. Dilys sensed that a relationship had ended for me but told me that there was someone around me—he was my Sir Lancelot—at first I couldn't place this man but a month or so later a close friend of mine looked at me in a certain way—it was magical. I fell madly, deeply in love and am now so happy in this union. This man who was my friend became my lover and we both recognize that we are soul-mates. Dilys said I would have a wonderful summer, full of languor, passion and love and I did. Thank you Dilys, love and light, Sara.

Tim and Carla sat down together for their reading. He was perhaps forty, rugged and marked by a tough life; she was a breathtaking twenty, with a Mediterranean beauty that was so perfect it was difficult to believe she was real, glossy black air and lusciousness of face and figure. I did not even have to look at the cards or take their hands.

'I hope you will not take this the wrong way, but I see in you both your own destinies,' I told them. 'Whatever happened to each of you before you met, is irrelevant. And my guess is that when you set eyes on each other there was immediate recognition.'

Smiling quietly, exchanging looks, they nodded.

'You were given this gift—each other—as something beyond ordinary happiness,' I said. 'Few people are granted the relationship that was waiting for you. It is a love that allows no questions, no queries, no mistrust or doubt. I think it transformed both your lives, changed all your plans, gave you a joy simply in being and being together.'

Smiling again, they nodded agreement, and I went on to read the cards for them, together in their separate—and yet joined—future. There was a sense of fulfilment in the patterns of their reading, of balance. There have been cases of other couples who have also been granted this gift and they all possess the same sense of stillness and calm, of existing apart and yet together, in a state where nothing needs to be added or disputed or even said.

'We felt we must have met in another life,' Carla told me impetuously.

'We knew each other—at least, I felt I knew her. I could hardly believe it when she ...' Tim seemed lost for words.

'You still doubt, I think. You find it difficult to accept,' I told him, and he nodded, with a little shrug.

'Her faith is greater than mine. I've knocked round the world and I'm not easily conned.'

'Do you think you are being conned?' I asked, smiling, and he grinned a crooked smile.

'If I am, I want to stay conned. But—you know what I mean.'

'There are miracles, there are great love stories—and there's Tim and Carla,' I said. 'It was meant. Accept it in simplicity. How did it happen, when your lives were going their separate ways, with other people involved? Ask questions and you will weaken the magic. Just believe.'

*   *   *

There are more secretive 'outsiders' who appear less often—in fact I have never had such a one come to me directly. They are the followers of 'black magic' rather than 'white', those drawn to evil and negative power rather than to the positive and the light. But occasionally the victims of dark forces make contact.

In Charmaine's case, she looked completely ordinary and sat through a reading for her sister, helping, consoling and giving strength and courage. Then they changed places. I held Charmaine's hands and concentrated.

'At some time, you have been close to the dark,' I said. This is the phrase I use when I know the sitter has been in contact with some form of 'black' or 'left-hand' activity. It is not possible to tell whether they have deliberately set out to practise 'black magic' themselves or have been a follower of someone who has, whether they have had dealings with demonic forces or been a victim. But if the sense of dark is around them, I know there has to be something. I can also pick up the presence of darkness which has been overcome, and from which they are currently free. Charmaine shrugged.

'You know what it's like when you are young—you mess around with things—the ouija board. I did have a bad time, but that was years ago.'

'You are very strong, you've got rid of all of it and there is nothing there now to cause you harm,' I said.

'I know,' she agreed grimly. 'It nearly killed me, but I did it and fought my way out.'

Leaving the topic, since it seemed nothing more than an old war she had waged successfully, I went on to do her reading, and when I laid out the cards, one of them, representing the Devil and with an image of the typical 'devilish' goat-headed monster on it, caught her eye. She touched it with her finger.

'My son has that tattooed on his chest.'

'Why? Does he like the idea of being a devil-worshipper?' I asked lightly. I always try to approach such subjects in a non-committal manner, since one never knows exactly what will emerge. Her reply, casually thrown across the cards, was shocking.

'I don't know about likes the idea. But his father was a devil-worshipper and I saw my son being ritually dedicated to Satan in a big ceremony when he was a baby.'

'You allowed it?' I asked, and she shrugged.

'What could I do? Even if I'd tried to argue. But sometimes now I feel this is our punishment, what we're getting. He's nineteen, and I love him—and he's dying and I'm going to lose him.'

'Not because of being dedicated to Satan,' I said, feeling my way.

'He's a heroin addict—or at least,' she corrected proudly, 'he was. He's just come clean, two weeks ago, after years. He's done it, done it himself. Finally done it.'

'Then?'

'He's got hepatitis B,' she said wearily. 'Nothing to be done. It's a matter of months.'

But it was a case of deep human tragedy now, rather than of struggling with the dark, and I gave her what comfort I would have given to any other mother who was facing up so bravely to the loss of her son.

*   *   *

In contrast to the followers of darkness, the 'Messiahs'—which is my own word for extremely enlightened souls who have some sort of mission to perform, some sort of lead to give or cosmic destiny marked out for them—arrive as Eric did, in 'clouds of glory'. Jeff had been aware of his destiny for as long as he could remember, recollected his near-death experience (which in some shape or form seems to characterize every person who has a link with the star planes, with extra-terrestrials or other worlds) and described not only that but the UFOs which used to visit him as a young boy, landing in the garden outside his bedroom window at night.

Through another 'Messiah', James, I was able to make contact with the race which had sent him, and communicate with them. Tall beings of light and knowledge, with no feelings, they were very different to the traditional bug-eyed monsters of science fantasy, but frightening at first in their utter coldness and the sense of being genuinely 'alien' to me.

Rather surprisingly, the 'Messiahs' I have encountered are often very vulnerable in so far as they are generally alone, contained within themselves and because of their awareness of their origins and destinies, subject to the same sense of alienation and 'difference' that an astronaut would feel if projected into a Venusian civilization with instructions to 'try and pretend you're one of them'.

Another interesting feature seems to uphold a type of cosmic 'male chauvinism', since although there are star children of both sexes, there are to my knowledge no female 'Messiahs'!

CHAPTER SEVEN

IN TOUCH

One of the most mystifying psychic powers to the uninitiated is known as psychometry. It means that the psychic can handle an object and can pick up vibrations from it which will reveal information or facts about the person who owned or wore it.

The earliest 'case' I ever had using psychometry was during a session within a circle for developing psychic powers. I was given, as a test, a ring belonging to a young woman. I picked up the most awful sense of pain, hurt, desolation, and I ventured the opinion that she had been abandoned as a child, or had been most brutally treated. I also seemed to pick up the sense of the entity lying deep in some sort of ditch, covered over with long grass. The feeling that accompanied these visions was so violent that it almost knocked me to the floor, and (unused to dealing with such cases) I felt unable to let the pain go or break away from it.

The owner of the ring rather defiantly denied all knowledge of what I had seen, but I found out later that someone close to her, perhaps a friend or within her family—I never know whether it had even involved herself—had recently suffered either an abortion or a miscarriage.

I was able to work out later when I had other such experiences to draw on, that what I had picked up was the brief moment of living awareness of the little spirit which had hardly touched the earth, hardly flickered before it was gone. I had tuned in as though to a looped tape repeating itself endlessly, of pain, bewilderment and uncomprehending fear.

126

Something indicated too that the case had involved the actual body of the hardly formed child being abandoned literally in a ditch and not being laid to rest, though of course I had no way of checking on this. But a young girl trying to cope alone, in pain and very frightened, might well have rid herself of all evidence of what had happened to her in a nearby ditch that would hide everything in its deep grass. This is not, unfortunately, an unfamiliar scenario.

*   *   *

Visitors to psychic fairs or members of the public generally are usually unaware of what psychometry is, but more enlightened sitters sometimes arrive with wedding rings or other jewellery which belonged to a relative—though by far the most common objects produced for examination in the cases I have dealt with have been snaps and pictures, usually of husbands or boyfriends, from which the ladies concerned want me to deduce whether 'he really loves me'. I personally find psychometry a very useful tool in this respect, as the snapshot generally confirms what I have already picked up clairvoyantly about the person who is pictured in it.

*   *   *

The most staggering case that I have ever

experienced involving pure psychometry did not happen in the line of duty, as it were, but casually. A friend who dealt in bric-à-brac handed me three heavy boxes, obviously old 'objects' and said: 'See what you get from these, just out of interest.'

The first was a set of medical instruments in a case, a 'do-it-yourself' diagnostic outfit for everything from earache to childbirth. The second was more dubious. It seemed to be some sort of early electric massager or even 'vibrator', though nobody could work out exactly how it could be put to beneficial use. The third seemed electrical also, and looked like a radio but was more likely, I was told, a type of generator.

I tried the medical instruments first, running my hands over the wooden lid. The picture that formed in my mind was of a district nurse in the 1940s, who had taken the box and its contents with her on her rounds, through a countryside that seemed to be filled with cottage gardens and sunlight, very dry in summer heat. I assumed that (not surprisingly) the box had been hers.

When I put my hands on the box containing the 'vibrator' I could do nothing but giggle. I had a picture of a hotel room—in an afternoon—but it was not very detailed, and what was coming through far more strongly was the great sense of exhilaration and fun that was sweeping me off my feet. I got the impression that the two people who had been together in the hotel room, and to whom the box had belonged, had made life very happy for each other—but they had not been able to work out what to do with the 'vibrator' either!

Then, unprepared and unsuspecting, I put my hands on the third and largest box. I was silent for several moments while the patterns began to form, then I said blankly: 'This can't be right. He's killing her.'

The images did not come in chronological order but in surging impressions. Often I can pick up whole chunks of quite detailed information in a fraction of a second. These were very vivid and I could feel myself becoming distressed; after about five minutes I pushed the box away and said I wanted nothing more to do with it. It took some time before I was able to overcome the distress I had felt and consider the situation rationally. I had picked up something very terrible and needed time to absorb the implications.

*　　*　　*

It was as though by touching the box I had started a film running, and I continued to pick up more and more information during the night and into the next morning. What I had witnessed was the murder of a young girl. The actual murder scene played itself over and over, but I was also able to fill in a great deal of background detail.

The setting seemed to have been a northern town in about the early fifties. I was not able to identify the town, except that I thought there was a nuclear power station or some sort of nuclear plant close by, and the town was situated near a river or large canal, where there was a towpath or similar path running alongside the water, and trees.

The murderer—the man who had owned the box—had not been local. He had come to the town and lived alone in a rented room, keeping himself to himself. He worked during the day at something innocuous like clerking in an office, but in the evenings, he spent his time in his room with this and other generators and equipment, seemingly, so far as I could gather, trying to harness the nuclear power so that he could use it for his own benefit to 'rule the world'. He did not mix with other people, and from what I could pick up of his mind and his fanatical ambitions, he seemed hardly sane.

The murder was pathetic and tragic. It had happened on the path near the water, under some trees, in the dark. I never saw the face of the victim, since she had been struck from behind, and I saw it from his viewpoint only, but I was able to tell that she had been young, with very fair hair, perhaps dyed and probably waved, about shoulder length. She was slight and had been completely taken by surprise so had not struggled at all. She had not known the murderer was there, she had been walking along the path and he had been walking behind her, his shoes very quiet, maybe rubber-soled. He always moved quietly.

He had hit her with something heavy, perhaps a stone, at the back of the neck, and she had fallen forward on to her face to lie there unmoving. I noticed that she was wearing a big loose coat with a big collar, and that she was carrying a handbag, which lay untouched beside her afterwards.

The information from the box continued to reveal itself in incredible detail. I knew from the murderer's mind that the crime had been something entirely unpremeditated. He happened to have been at that spot at that time, he did not know the girl but there was a well of twisted passion within him—linked to his desire for power and his feelings of 'difference' and superiority—and something about her youth and vulnerability, her innocence, had touched a deeply hidden nerve within him. Before he knew what he had done, she was lying there at his feet.

It had been as simple as that.

But once the deed was done, he knew he had to leave the town immediately, and I saw him return to his room, pack and settle his affairs. I saw him catching the train for London and arriving there to be lost in the crowds. He was never caught. The murder was never solved, and he died alone, years later.

I could not get the name or identity of the girl, but two names came to me in connection with the murderer—Ronald Ernest or Ernest Ronald. I always meant to try and follow this case up, but I have never had the time or opportunity. Somewhere, though, gathering dust, the still open file on this particular murder exists. It was never solved because there was no apparent motive, no connection between the girl and the man who murdered her. But the murderer's box, which he later sold to a pawnbroker and which made its way by a long and roundabout route into the possession of my friend the dealer, had carried the solution with it and, when I held it in my hands, was able to reveal the answer to me.

*　　*　　*

Psychometry has—generally unofficially—been able to assist with solving crimes, and though I have never been called in to use my powers to help solve criminal cases I have been able to form my own 'answers' for cases which have baffled or mystified the authorities. Take the case of the Fulham estate agent Suzy Lamplugh who disappeared on 28 July 1986. I have almost no knowledge or recollection of the incident itself, but by running my fingers over a copy of her name, I pick up most strongly the word 'salt', which may mean real salt, or be symbolic or a name significant to her

132

disappearance in some way.

I further feel that electrodes or electric apparatus—perhaps a slimming machine, or the medical treatment of electro-convulsive therapy, for example (the latter does cause a certain amount of memory 'loss')—have some connection with this case, though it is impossible to be more specific. I also sense that whatever has happened after her disappearance, she is still alive, that many know about the truth of the matter though it is not publicly acknowledged and that she has either been or is currently, in another country.

From these impressions I have gained from her name (and names give off extremely strong and powerful vibrations), it would be impossible for me to present a solution to this baffling and upsetting case. I have no idea of what significance a slimming machine or any other sort of electrical equipment might have nor who was responsible for abducting her—if she was abducted—or why. Neither does that very clear word 'salt' mean anything at all to me in this case. But, as always with psychic vision, the psychic must give exactly what he sees. To someone with more information these few impressions could help to clarify the whole situation.

Psychometry is one of the most spectacular ways to illustrate psychic ability when a psychic is asked to do a 'demonstration' of his or her work. In fact, if one is not careful it can get out of hand. A typical demonstration of this type, of which I do many in the course of psychic fairs or other public appearances, will consist of an informal gathering of some twenty or thirty people sitting in a half-circle, while I stand or sit in the middle. My opening gambit is to explain briefly what psychometry involves, how the 'vibrations' which cling to material things can be responsible for a sense of inexplicable happiness when handling some particular object, to the 'haunted' and depressing atmosphere that can still pervade a place where there was an intensity of tragic or despairing emotion. Then I move on to the demonstration, and ask for someone in the audience to give me a personal item that is their own and has belonged to no one else. Invariably these are rings, necklaces or watches.

The most usual reactions I get from this quick handling of items are of a superficial kind—that the people concerned are very stressed, have perhaps been ill recently, are worried on behalf of someone else—'you're waiting for some important news, from abroad, I think—yes?—well, it's on its way—and the news is good'—'You are a person who has given to others all your life, but now you need to think of yourself'. As soon as one reading has been done, there are eager hands holding out another twenty rings and watches wanting their turn, and I try to cover as many as I can, for it is just possible that there may be someone in real need, though generally the audience is just curious and has few serious problems that cannot be coped with in the ordinary run of events.

One such session brought me a ring which belonged to a seemingly self-possessed young woman. I turned it in my fingers.

'You have just suffered a very heavy bereavement.'

'Yes,' she said quietly, giving nothing away.

'When?'

'Last Thursday. My mother.'

I gave her the ring back and told her I would see her privately afterwards. This sort of pain is too personal to use as part of any demonstration.

A particularly drum-rolling item of psychometry is to ask for a single human hair to be placed in one's hand without even seeing whether it has come from the head of a man or a woman, and to proceed to tell the audience about the 'owner'. What can be embarrassing, however, is when—as invariably happens— secrets are revealed which the people concerned deny emphatically. I picked up from one lady's hair during a demonstration that she had a very passionate nature, and that any man who was close to her would live in a state of perpetual sexual fascination. When I put this across—tactfully, I thought—it still met with maidenly blushes as though I had said something indelicate to the vicar's wife—though what I had seen about the lady's real character was so vividly explicit that the scenes conjured up would never have been granted a certificate for release!

Another time I said the hair had come from the head of a lady, and it turned out to belong to a young man. He was not a homosexual, but possessed a particularly sweet and gentle nature. I explained this as clearly as I could, adding that what I had picked up was in fact simply a feminine gentleness and feminine strength, and I had assumed the hair belonged to a woman. He accepted this quite happily, but the subtleties arising from what is given, or the way in which it is given, do sometimes need explanation or deeper investigation, and I usually regard psychometry as something to cross-check with, especially if there seems to be any doubt or confusion.

*   *   *

In some cases, however, psychometry works very well and is extremely effective. Shara, a self-assured career woman who had already approached me with a view to including me in a television film she wanted to make about the spiritual nature of psychic work in England, the USA and her native India, consulted me about a friend who had recently undergone a series of severe traumas concerning a court case affecting his personal life, and who seemed to have withdrawn completely into himself.

'I cannot get through to him,' she told me. 'He will not even see me, not talk to me, and we were so close.' She gave me a snapshot. 'This is him. Can you get anything from it?'

I did not look at the face in the picture, but touched the surface gently, concentrating hard. Images began to form.

'This man is a prisoner, I see him within a cave-like place which is utterly dark,' I said. 'He is sitting on the ground with his knees pulled up and his head bent, trying to escape from his own reality. There is no window, but there is a door, and if he wanted to, he could open it, but that is the last thing he wants at the moment.'

'You mean he is really in some place like that?'

'No, it is his mind I am linking to,' I said. 'His body is probably performing everyday tasks without trouble. But his mind is alone in the dark.'

'It makes sense,' she said slowly.

'I am also picking up a scene—this man believes in romance and magic, in fairy-stories.' She nodded. 'He has been damaged by a wicked queen who was threatening him, and I see a scene where he is running down a long flight of very wide stairs, a curving staircase, with a child held closely in his arms. He is trying to escape from the wicked queen and save the child. This probably did not happen, of course, but that is how he regards the things that have passed, it is symbolic of his feelings.'

Shara was looking serious. 'I think you must be right, because what you have described sums up exactly the sort of situation which he has just gone through, what the court case was all about. But if he has shut himself away in this dark place, what shall I do? How can I help him?'

'You must let him have the rest he needs, just wait for the time being.'

'He has passed on messages to wait,' she said worriedly.

'He needs time. At least give him time. People do not get over traumas at the same rate, and he is a very sensitive man.'

She agreed, after further discussion, to let the situation alone for the time being, but in another few weeks she asked me to do a further reading. There had apparently been some small moves on either side, and she wanted to know whether his state of mind was still the same.

As soon as I touched the picture I was able to tell her that 'the door is open. He is still inside the cave but the door is open and when he is ready he will come out.'

'What shall I do?' she asked eagerly. 'Shall I go to see him? Write to him?'

'No,' I told her. 'He was put into this

situation by magic—the way he sees it—with the wicked queen driving him to escape down that long, long flight of stairs in the dark, clutching the child. He feels there have been spells and counter spells, and only magic will save him. You need to create some magic of your own and approach him in a roundabout way.'

She nodded. 'Again, I see the sense. But how can I create magic?'

'Whatever will seem magical to him. A rose. A valentine. A lock of hair. Anything he will feel represents true love. Sent anonymously. He has been in the cold with the dark magic—he needs the warmth of the magic of true love to bring him out through that door.'

*   *   *

There were further meetings and consultations after that, and Shara told me at one of them, when I arrived, that the photograph which I had used each time had changed. The face, she declared, had started off looking worried and gloomy—it had changed and now appeared brighter and full of hope. I could not tell whether this was so myself, because my vision of all my sitters is often extremely changeable. For instance, when a sitter takes a seat opposite to me and I spend half an hour or so in conversation with them, I often find that when the sitting is over and they rise to leave, I see

139

their face quite differently from the way I have been looking at it during the sitting.

I find as they leave that they may look older, harder, sharper, that lines which I had not noticed are visible. The only way in which I can account for this is to assume that because the sitting is generally on a very close level—often 'soul to soul', as it were—I do not actually see the outer body clearly until the session is over. This would link up with the change in the physical body at the time of death, when the marks of age, suffering and pain are wiped away as though they have never been. The soul, whether released by physical death, or revealed to me or any other psychic, is ageless, pure and infinitely beautiful.

Shara agreed in principle about the magical and delicate approach, and everything I had told her about her friend's feelings and what had caused them. She regarded my insight into his state of mind as remarkable, especially as other investigation proved I was probably, so far as anyone could tell, completely accurate. But I felt my suggestions were clashing with her own strong views on how best to handle the situation, and although I heard later that the gentleman in question had left the country to work in America, I never knew whether she managed to reach him with the magic, and resolve their difficulties.

*   *   *

On other occasions, sitters have produced snapshots of lost pets and asked desperately where they can be found. Roma had a snap of 'Chewy', a black-and-white cat. I asked whether he had previously roamed for days at a time, and she said he had. I picked up something that looked like a large rubbish tip, and asked whether there was one near her home. Yes, there was. She volunteered the information that there was also an old quarry, a deserted railway and a lot of waste land.

My feeling on holding the picture, was that Chewy was probably at the tip, and that he had accidentally slid down a small distance of only a foot or so, perhaps on loose rubbish or shale, but had been unable to climb out of the hole or hollow where he found himself. I advised her to go there and call to him, so that, on hearing her voice, he would respond. Otherwise it seemed that she might be within only a few feet of him but he would not know she was there, and equally, she would not be aware of him and could not lift him that vital foot or so.

'I'll go now,' she breathed. 'Straight away.'

Yet strangely enough, she was back at the fair in only an hour or so, asking another psychic about his whereabouts. I learned afterwards that this time she had been told Chewy was probably in the railway cutting, and was in no danger. Whatever action she took in the end, it seemed likely that— wherever her pet was, and whatever different vision each psychic obtained—the chances were that he was going to turn up yet again after his 'roamabout' by whatever strange fluke of circumstances.

In a case like this, I could give no guarantee that he was at the rubbish tip, only that I was receiving indications that she should go there and make sure she continued to call to him, as I could 'see' him below ground level. The person who told her Chewy was at the railway cutting was receiving a vision of his own. The question of faith enters very much into the scheme of things, for those who continue to make the rounds of psychics in search of corroboration or 'proof' or something definitive are looking for the impossible. The psychic world does not work that way.

What might, however, have happened, if Roma had had the faith to follow the advice I was given for her, was that on the way to the tip, or even at the tip, or possibly after making a search there and finding nothing, but carrying out her instructions in good faith, she would have found Chewy restored to her either of his own accord or by the means I had indicated or because someone else had found him somewhere else. This might sound like pure chance, that would in all probability have happened anyway, but by coming to me she had set in motion a chain of events which would have depended on her own faith. Faith can work miracles, but equally, if there is no faith there is no point in asking for help and then rejecting it and going somewhere else. The psychometry in this case meant she had to take things just as much on trust, whichever psychic she consulted—and if Chewy was going to free himself anyway and return home within a few days, whatever anyone said about his current whereabouts was equally relevant or irrelevant. She never bothered to inform any of us whether he did come back or not.

*   *   *

Another odd case concerned a man who gave his name as Todd. He sat down, produced a photograph of a pretty woman and asked me whether I could tell him where she was. Something was wrong somewhere, and I prevaricated with a few questions.

'What's her name, please?'

'Pat—Patricia.'

'Is she your wife?'

'No.'

'Any relation?'

'No.'

'You just want to know where she is. As a friend.'

'Absolutely. As a friend.'

I held the picture experimentally.

'She isn't dead—is she?'

He shrugged. 'I don't think so.'

'No, she's alive. But she is not in this

143

country. She's on a train at the moment, travelling somewhere between Switzerland, Austria, Germany, that area.'

'On a train.' He nodded slowly. 'Where is she going?'

'I don't know. I've told you the area. Has she relatives there? Might she be on holiday?'

He shrugged again, impatiently. 'I've no idea. You can see no more than that?'

I could, but I did not tell him so. I could see that his intentions towards Patricia were violently and cruelly possessive, that if he found her he would do her harm.

'When did you see her last?' I asked.

'A few weeks ago,' he said.

It figured. I saw that he regarded Patricia as his property but that she had at last broken away. I could feel her fear and panic. This man was of the kind who would stalk his prey, his possession, across the face of the earth and never let go. I sent her what encouragement and strength I could, knowing that though she was indeed travelling away to make a new life for herself, he might pursue her for years, always only a few steps behind. But he would not catch her yet. And I was reluctant to give him any further assistance. I handed the picture back and told him I was sorry but I was unable to help.

'I have to find her, you see,' he said by way of explanation. 'I must find her. She is my whole life.'

Obsession? Possession? All I knew was that I was silently willing Patricia's train to hurry, even as I was courteously saying goodbye to the hunter who stalked her.

CHAPTER EIGHT

THE GIFT OF HEALING

Luisa is a tough, half-caste lesbian. She came to me first in a state of despair, having just suffered the latest in a series of betrayals—her partner had just left her for her ex-lover, who had previously left her for someone else. The brave façade she was giving out to the people she worked with, the 'damn your eyes' exterior, was hiding a heart that had been cruelly damaged and might have been, to coin a phrase 'broken'. Except that hearts cannot break. They just feel as though they are broken and the pain can be indescribable.

When Luisa came to me again, some six months or so later, she was a different person. No longer gaunt and hag-ridden, but with a new confidence in herself and a sense of peace about her. She was smiling, and the hug she gave me to say 'hello' was warm and genuine.

Whatever I had been able to give Luisa— whatever had passed to her through me at the time of our first sitting—had been a form of healing. And though often the healing I give is not easy to define, I see the results in the faces of sitters who come back to me. Some of them, like Marie, are on their way, their feet safely on the path. Others have slipped or fallen and need support to go forward again. Luisa was making steady progress.

When I am asked whether I make a tape recording of sittings, I reply that I do not. This is because I feel it is the whole experience, everything that is said, felt, expressed, revealed and acknowledged on both sides, that matters, the half-hour or so that my sitter and I spend together. The words, out of their context, can be useful but lose their impact—and in any case, the mind will not forget anything that matters. Somewhere, it will be retained until the time is right.

Sherri, who had a sitting with me where we explored many of her emotional problems as well as consulting the cards for her future, wrote to me in August 1994: 'I felt it was a complete healing experience for me.' This is a great tribute, but it expresses something I aim for constantly—to make each sitting a healing process for my sitter as well as deal with the more trivial queries like: 'Will I travel?' and 'Will I marry?' and 'Will I be successful?'

*   *   *

As a healer, I work intuitively, though I am

well aware that I use methods borrowed from many traditional forms of healing, including, often, psychology and basic forms of counselling. I can also heal by touch, the power in my hands. On many occasions I have taken the hands of a sitter and found that their overwhelming need—as opposed to the strength of the power itself, which is always there—has almost dragged the force down my arms and out through my hands.

In cases like this, the effect is of a river running so fast that the channels through which it is flowing are threatened, and my arms and shoulders, sometimes my whole body, is violently shaken. In fact, though, the giving of healing takes nothing from the healer except the ordinary effort that would go into any work, and I feel rested and restored myself after giving healing.

*   *   *

As a healer, I see no such thing as 'sick' or 'well'. I see my ideal, what I want to give my sitters, in wholeness, and this includes physical, emotional and spiritual harmony and balance. So I heal often on different levels.

When Luisa arrived, she was worn and tired. She was very distressed, distraught, suffering from the complicated reactions to her various rejections, her self-esteem at an extreme low, needing a great deal of support to lift her and carry her forward. The first thing I did was take her hands. Until I have held the hand of a sitter, I cannot always link in deeply, but when I touch their hands I can pick up most kinds of illness and am able to judge whether there is a need for healing. If there is, I deal with that first.

Sometimes I will ask: 'Have you been ill recently?' or 'You've just had an operation, haven't you?' Usually the physical ailments of this sort are on the mend, but occasionally someone has confronted me uncompromisingly with the presence of human mortality. Ursula, for instance, sat down at one psychic fair and said bluntly:

'It's my husband. He's dying. I want to know how long he has left and when he's going to go.'

I looked at her sharply. I saw suns and moons, the shifting layers of immense wisdom and knowledge, within her eyes. I knew she had to be right, it was no use telling her there was always hope, or something I might have said to someone less aware.

'I'm not worried at all, of course,' she said. 'I know there is nothing to worry about. But I am going to be left and I'd like to know how much longer we have before this particular parting. I'd also like to be reassured, if this is possible, that he will not suffer.'

We spent her sitting discussing the irrelevancy of death in the great scheme of things, wandering—as she was sure she and her husband would continue to do—in the great unity of the Absolute, where there is no time and no awareness of anything except the simplicity of simply being. At the end, still as brisk and no-nonsense as she had been when she sat down, she rose declaring she felt much better and left abruptly.

Oddly enough, at the same fair on the same day, another lady, Doris, broached the subject of death. Another psychic, she declared, had told her that her husband did not have long to live, and though there did not seem to be anything wrong with him, she was worried and wanted to know if I could help. She did not think she could manage if he were to die, she said, she didn't think she could stand it.

When I looked into the situation, I saw that her husband was indeed going to die quite soon, in a car accident on an icy road. I also saw that she would be with him and neither of them would survive. It was going to happen around the next Christmas time. I also saw that nothing could be done to stop it, so the most healing thing I was able to do was to reassure her that 'whenever the time came, and none of us can alter that', they would go together, and it would be sudden so there would be no question of suffering or of one of them having to survive the other.

'Don't worry about it,' I said. 'Just take each day as it comes. If we all worried all the time about when we were going to die, we would have no life at all. Enjoy today, and don't worry about the bad things that might come along tomorrow—wait until they happen. They might never come at all.'

*   *   *

I have encountered spiritual healers who work in a similar way to the way I work—by invoking and forming a channel for the power and strength of the spirit, the light, whatever one calls it—who claim they can actually 'cure' such physical ailments as cancer and wearing away of bones. I do not deal with physical illness on this scale, and never make any claims that I can 'cure' anything, though the peace and serenity, the relaxation and hope and positivity that a session of healing can bring, is often the tip, as it were, of the iceberg, and it is possible to see a huge upsurge of general well-being in a patient as a result. If their emotional and physical problems are sorted out—to whatever degree—as well, the effect can often seem like a 'miracle-cure'.

*   *   *

Back to Luisa, whose case is guiding us through this chapter. As I held her hands, feeling her depletion of energy and hope and sense of worth and self, I knew she was receiving healing through my grasp, and would feel stronger and more positive afterwards. I continued to hold her hands while I encouraged her to talk about her situation.

In her case, I felt the real healing she needed was to be able to realize that the women who had treated her so badly were her inferiors and that she would be able to find the love and happiness she needed in a more positive situation when she felt an equal. She had to discover her own strength, her own ability to transcend the petty rivalries among her current 'friends' and lift herself, in fact, to the higher level where she belonged.

We must have talked of so many things, but one recommendation I made to her was to try and get away to make contact with herself, her own person, and to learn to be proud of that person. When I saw her later, looking so much more vibrant, she told me she had taken my advice, and went down regularly to a cottage she owned in the West Country, where she was free to 'find herself'.

'There's a big menhir, some sort of ancient stone, not far away, and I discovered a long, lonely walk that takes me to it,' she said. 'I'm alone with my Higher Self, with just the sky and the sea and the trees. And—.' She gave me a sidelong glance, laughing. 'I have found a real friend—instead of the others, you know?'

I nodded encouragingly. 'The lady you shared the cottage with?'

'No. No lady. As I go along this walk, there's

a special tree. I put my arms round it and talk to it, and . . .'

'You don't have to tell me. It talks back to you. Gives you advice, sorts things out for you. Makes you feel loved and wanted and unique. The real Luisa, part of the universe.' I tell her sincerely how glad I am that she has discovered the key of healing and enlightenment for herself. 'Because you will have this awareness and strength with you always now. Nothing will ever be able to take it away.'

*   *   *

Apart from the incidental healing which occurs in a sitting from coping with the problems of the sitter, I give various actual 'healing sessions' if the person requires it. Nearly every sitter who comes to me needs healing of some sort, but few ask for it. If you translate 'healing' as 'guidance towards wholeness' this strange ignorance of their need is easier to understand. Very few people have any sense at all that they want or need to aim for 'wholeness' in their personalities and their lives.

*   *   *

Abby's case illustrates how a 'healing session' works. She arrived at the venue where I was working, in search of the spiritual healer in the same building, who was not there that day. When she found she was unable to have a session of spiritual healing, she was distressed, and I offered to give her a healing session instead, though I do not describe myself as a spiritual healer—simply as a healer, the methods of which might be many and varied, whatever is most effective.

She sat down gratefully. I picked up a cloud of depressive negativity and tiredness around her. She had a fine, psychic spirit which was wearing very thin, and I set to work.

For a 'healing session' I usually follow a pattern I have evolved over a period of time, which seems to bring rest, calm, strength and upliftment, and I applied this in Abby's case.

Smoothing the 'aura', invisible to the human eye but which I can sense about six inches away from the body, releasing tangles and snarls round the head and hair, I said quietly: 'I just want you to close your eyes and relax. Let the tension go. Listen to my voice, you'll hear what I say and all the rest of the sounds around will fade into the background.'

The next step was to place the back of my hand gently on her abdomen as I continued to talk soothingly. 'I want you to take a deep breath, right down into the bottom of your lungs. See if you can make my hand rise. There—breathe right in—and hold for a few seconds—and let it go, all the tension and stress, a big sigh. And now again—breathe right in—hold for a few seconds—and let it all go.'

I repeated this two or three times—no more—and continued to talk as I massaged the back of her neck and the shoulders, pressing deeply into the tense muscles and ridding them of their stress. 'This is just for you, just for yourself, a few minutes when you don't have to think, worry about anybody else. Let all the worries and the stresses and the dark and the tension go, leave them behind. Just listen to my voice and the murmurs in the background and relax. There is absolutely nothing to worry about, nothing to be afraid of.'

By now, Abby, typically, was beginning to breathe regularly and relax in a light trance. I went on to the next step. Cupping my hands at the top of her head I said (though I do not use involvement of the chakras, energy points of the body, beyond this point): 'At the top of your head is the Crown Chakra, like the tightly curled petals of a lotus flower. Imagine the flower opening up, the petals are opening like the fingers of my hands, opening out and down into your head is coming the most beautiful pure white light. See the light filling the dark spaces within you, going down into your head and every part of your body, cleansing and purifying and refining you and filling every corner, so there is no single bit of dark or worry or stress left anywhere.'

While I encouraged her to concentrate on

154

the light flooding through and bringing strength and positivity, I smoothed and calmed the aura round her upper body. As I did so, I continued with further visualization. 'I want you to imagine that your chair has left the ground and floated up into the sky—the most beautiful blue sky—and beyond the blue, there is gold light too, as far as you can see, and as well as the silver light. You are drifting, gently drifting, so peacefully amid the colours—blue is the colour of healing. Just let go and drift...'

I held each of her hands in turn for several moments for healing comes, as I have said, through my own hands.

'And while you are drifting, you feel, just gently, the touch of tiny snow-flakes on your hair, on your face. But they are not snow-flakes, they are star-flakes, the most lovely and minute fragments of silver, little bits of star, covering you and tangling in your hair.' My hands weaved the star-flakes round her head. 'They will be there when you go, all around you, so pure and fine and beautiful, to give you hope and comfort and serenity and protect you with their beauty.'

I worked on these images a little further, and induced more calm. Sometimes I use the images of water—a waterfall and a riverbed of tiny pebbles which are in fact shining gem-stones of amethyst, crystal, emerald, ruby, and anything else that seems appropriate, to be gathered up and taken forward to give the same sort of hope, strength and enlightenment to my sitter. If I detect any particular weakness I will do specific healing for it. And towards the end, I 'lift' the sitter by touching the shoulders, to a healing plane. Some sitters do not comment on this, as they are not aware of it, but others—Abby was one—tell me afterwards that 'I left my body, I was flying' or more specifically, 'I went to the place where the doves are—it was so beautiful.'

When the session has reached its natural end, I bring the sitter safely back to the body, and prepare to bring the session to a close.

'Now I am closing down the Crown Chakra, see the petals shutting tightly, to keep that beautiful silver light in, and all the dark outside. Feel the petals closing.' I closed them with my hands, tightly together on the top of the head. 'And now your chair is floating back, floating gently back and you are sitting here with me. And when you are ready, you will open your eyes.'

*   *   *

The result in Abby's case as well as with most patients, is a slow return to awareness, an involuntary smile, sometimes from those who have never experienced this sort of healing before, a dazed: 'Wow, I feel so odd. Light-headed'. Or 'I just don't know what happened, I seem to have been floating in all those glorious lights for hours.' Or 'I swear I was out of my body, I was somewhere else.'

The healer has to be extremely responsible for the safety and protection of the patient while administering this type of healing. It is also very necessary when putting someone into even the lightest of trances to relax them, that no loophole is left open through which control can be lost or any type of distress be caused. The patient is in the healer's hands, in faith and trust, often in ignorance of the person he or she is entrusting themselves to, and what that person will do or is capable of doing.

Abby hugged me after her session and said she felt so much better. A few weeks later, in December 1993, she sent me a card where she had written: 'I floated home after your healing with "snow-flakes" falling on my hair.' We had also talked, and she added: 'Thank you so much for the spontaneous past-life, it shifted the black cloud. I slept for twelve hours and felt so refreshed afterwards.'

The 'black cloud' in question had concerned Abby's leg, which was painful and did not function properly. I saw as we talked that this related to a past life where she had been the daughter of an industrialist in the north of England—and she had taken very much to heart the hardship of the workers at her father's cotton mill. In particular, one young girl had been caught in the machinery and lost a leg. Abby had taken it upon herself to compensate for this tragedy by 'giving' her own leg in her current life, even though she had not been responsible for the accident. She had tried to carry karmic blame herself, and I assured her that there was no way in which this would help, and that she must let it go.

'You can't carry the world on your shoulders,' I told her. 'Nobody can. Stop feeling responsible. It was past history, leave it be. You have suffered enough already—and to no real purpose. Choosing to suffer alongside someone else and cry with them does nothing to take their pain away, so be thankful for your own good fortune and health and make the most of it. That way you will lift others, rather than allow them to drag you down.'

People generally come to see me as a healer in one of two frames of mind. Some have utter, child-like faith that they will receive what they need; others are not sure what they will receive but have not found what they need by more conventional methods and are willing to take a chance. None of them expects miracles—in my experience as a psychic, sitters are far more surprised if the psychic is accurate than if they are given pointless generalities. They rarely complain that comments or predictions did not prove correct, but they will go to a great deal of trouble to make contact in delighted amazement to tell me, 'You were right, you said so-and-so would happen, and in April, and *it did*!'

Incredibly, my experience is that sitters do not really expect the psychic to be accurate and helpful. If they find more than the bland 'patter' they half-expected, they are thrilled and feel this is a bonus.

In the same way, sitters who come for healing do not expect miracle cures, or even to be 'healed' at all, and quite often they are staggered and overwhelmed when they receive something real and positive. Often, sitters are looking for something which might be quite basic, but which they have been unable to find elsewhere. They may not know exactly what they need.

*   *   *

Abby was trying to suffer for the 'sins of the fathers' quite literally, and her sense of relief when she was able to feel the burden being lifted from her was something that no one who has not felt the weight of guilt and 'sin' and their accompanying doubts, fears and sense of worthlessness and inadequacy, falling from their shoulders, as the heavy pack in *Pilgrim's Progress* tumbled to the ground, can ever appreciate.

This has nothing to do with belief or religion. Often the healing the sitter requires is no more than a sense of recognition as an individual, of being given an awareness that one still exists, one is actually involved in the great patterns of living, that one is a part of things.

*   *   *

Patrick sat down stiffly.

'My back,' he explained. 'I—it seems ridiculous for someone of my age to feel—well, shy—but I don't like people to know I wear a corset.'

I smiled at the tough, greying figure.

'I have the same problem,' I said, 'with my back. A lesion, the osteopath calls it, though I think myself it was an arrow I took when I was an English yeoman fighting out in the Holy Land during the Crusades. I feel just the same because I have to wear a corset though.'

Patrick had no expectation that I could 'cure' his back. But as I held his hands, I picked up anxiety and worry. He told me that he had just had an operation for cancer, and had been told it had been entirely successful.

'That seems right to me,' I said. 'I pick up no signs of potential serious illness now, in fact I am getting the impression you are a really tough guy, with a long way to go yet. But you are stressed and tense, and I will give you some healing in a moment, to help you relax. I suggest you take a break or a holiday if you can, and try to adjust to the fact that you are simply not an invalid any longer. You are— apart from the corset—still very much in the

160

land of the living, and very healthy.'

He revealed that he and his longtime partner Alec were to leave the following day for a tour of the Far East, and I picked up that a great deal of his worry had been in case reassurances about his health were inaccurate, and he 'disgraced himself' as an English gentleman by dying on the way, or having a relapse and adding to the problems he felt he had already given Alec, who had looked after him faithfully during his period of illness.

'You will feel much better once you get away from the surroundings where you feel you have been, and treated as, a sick person for so long,' I assured him. 'Try to think of yourself as just as healthy as anyone else, feel free to give yourself this rest and holiday. Enjoy the beautiful places and scenes you're going to see. Slow down. Take things as they come. So long as you take reasonable care, you will find you are far tougher than you think.'

I gave him a session of healing and at the end of the sitting he smiled. 'I didn't know why I was coming here, but I am very glad now that I did. I feel I can just look forward to the trip and believe there is still life left to me.'

*   *   *

Julia was another case whose need was for reassurance. She sat down looking harassed and careworn in spite of her attractive clothes and hairdo and softly pretty make-up. There were lines etched at the sides of her mouth. When I took her hands, I said:

'You have been very close to death, haven't you?'

'A big heart by-pass operation,' she said. 'But it's all over now.'

'Yes,' I said, much as I had said to Patrick. 'But you feel you are still an invalid, still trapped in the scenario of hospitals and tests and illness, don't you? And I think the thing that bothers you most is that all the people who love you find it difficult to forget what you have been through and they can't treat you in an ordinary manner.'

'They smother me,' she said in a low tone. 'I feel they dare not let me alone for a minute—my husband hovers all the time—I know they mean well, but it stifles me.'

'Have you thought why they do that?' I asked her. 'It's because every time your husband looks at you, now, lovely and full of life, he remembers the days of the operation and he thinks to himself "My God, I nearly lost her!" And he wants to sweep you into his arms and hold you close out of sheer thankfulness because he *didn't* lose you. When people have come that close to disaster they find it difficult to take their blessings for granted any more.'

'You think so?' she asked.

'Well, just put yourself in his place. How would you feel if you had been afraid you were going to lose him; when everything was over, you'd look at him and see that he was still there, but healthier and more himself than ever?'

'Yes,' she said rather dazedly. 'I see what you mean. I suppose I would want to be over-protective.' She considered for a moment. 'Yes, of course, I'd be so thankful, so afraid it was all a dream. Maybe I would be worse than he is. I'd never let him go. You're right.'

'And of course, you yourself are feeling you want to leave all that behind you. You have a life ahead, and you don't want to spend it in a wheelchair, being wrapped round in shawls. You want to be adventurous, go scaling a few peaks in the highlands, learn scuba-diving and explore some coral reefs, do all the things you thought you would never be able to do as an active woman. You have a great desire here in your cards to live—to enjoy being alive, being attractive, being—if you'll forgive me—sexy. And why not? As we've just said, when you have nearly lost something, the realization that you still have it is twice as sweet.'

She nodded eagerly. 'Maybe not the scuba-diving, but I do wish I could feel confident that I could be normal, do ordinary things. But ...' her face clouded, 'they say I will be all right, that there's no need to worry, but...'

'You do worry. Secretly. And you get impatient when your husband and family worry too. Because what you really want is not

163

sympathy and concern, but the reassurance that it is all over and you are going to be all right.'

'Yes. I didn't know whether I would live or die. I suppose I prepared myself for death in a sort of way, and the fact that I'm alive...'

'It's a situation you half-resent, if you're honest.'

She lowered her voice.

'Yes, I do. I feel like I don't know where I am. It was traumatic—to be so close to death—and now to be back in the real world again—and yet everybody treating me as though I might break...'

We spent her sitting discussing her confused emotions. Julia needed to feel she had her directions clear and that she was heading for a new and exciting phase of her life. I reassured her that she seemed healthy and with no problems I could pick up. There was nothing to stop her setting herself new ambitions, new goals, and going forward as a 'whole' person instead of a victim. By the time she left me, she was looking good—even better than when she had arrived, with a new sense of vivacity and purpose. Just a few words and a little encouragement had set her feet on the path. The rest, I told her, and knew I was right, she could and would do for herself.

CHAPTER NINE

WRITTEN IN THE CARDS

Rowena was with two friends, having a reading that was causing them a good deal of enjoyment. We had dealt with her past—not very exciting—'You just seemed to miss out on everything, I think', I said, which set them all nodding. A marriage which had gone sour— 'Well, what else could you expect with a wimp like Ken?' as her friends had sympathized. Then I laid out the cards which dealt with her present and future. She had no current job, no prospects, no on-going relationship.

'Do you know any foreigners?' I asked her. 'There is a man who seems to be Greek coming into your life, very good-looking. A whirlwind romance. I think he has some connection with a restaurant—you may get a job working there, but he's not just an employee. His family owns it—or else he owns it, or part-owns it.'

'I can't wait,' she breathed.

'Latin lovers are the best, Ro,' giggled her friend, Sheila.

I turned over three more cards and examined them carefully, then told her: 'According to what the cards tell me, you are going to meet a handsome foreigner—at a Greek restaurant, it appears—and be swept off your feet. His family will adore you and give you all the love and affection you need so much, make you feel wanted. And your future lies somewhere warm and Mediterranean—a Greek island, I think. You will marry and spend your time helping your husband to run a taverna near the beach. You'll feel young again, and deliriously happy.'

There was silence.

'It's just too good to be true,' she breathed.

'It is written here very clearly.'

'Just like that film—what was it—*Shirley Valentine*,' said Sheila enviously.

'Is it really going to happen?' Rowena asked me, and I said:

'The cards are never, but never wrong. I am human and I may interpret them wrongly. I am fallible and I may make mistakes, but what they reveal is always the truth. It does appear from this spread, taken at its face value, as though you have no worries, you are going to live a fairy-tale existence in the sun. But in fact, this whole spread, everything in it is suspect. I have to examine it very closely because, as Sheila has just said, it reads so like a fairy-tale, the plot of a film, the answer to all your problems just turning up out of the blue. It's perfectly possible that you might marry a handsome Greek and spend the rest of your life in the sun—far stranger things than that have happened. But I'm afraid all my instincts tell me that this whole scenario has to be

166

discounted. This is a picture created out of your feelings of dissatisfaction with the state of your life, you have overlaid the cards with imagination and dreams, produced something which would solve all your problems and bring sunshine into your life. I am afraid there is nothing of your real future here, except your longing for romance and colour and something—or someone—to brighten your day-to-day existence.

'But now that we have recognized these unrealistic dreams for what they are, let's examine the reality—what could really be there for you in the future.'

*   *   *

To many sitters the tarot cards themselves seem to symbolize the psychic powers. Some people are wary of them and ask for readings 'without the cards'. Others seem to feel that it is the cards themselves which provide the insight and the magic.

Both of these ideas are inaccurate, when, as in my own case, clairvoyance is involved. I have given many readings without the use of the cards; but when I do use them, it is only to help focus the clairvoyance and make my awareness sharper. And amazingly often—as in the case of Rowena—I find that the sitter's own feelings, wishes or desires can 'block off' the message I am receiving, and I need not only to interpret the clairvoyance coming to me via the cards, but to take into account the deceptive images my sitter is giving out, often in the form of a sort of 'smoke screen'.

In the end, though, it is not possible to hide any secrets from clairvoyance and the cards. When I lay out a spread, I will see details which I know are the truth, however much my sitter may deny them. As an inexperienced beginner one is tempted to believe the sitter who replies, in answer to a comment: 'Oh, no, it was not like that at all.' But when a psychic has gained confidence and experience, he or she will know the vision—in some way—is correct and say: 'That is what I see. I think I am right.'

I have never known a case where the cards—or my clairvoyant view through them—actually turned out to be wrong in this type of situation.

*   *   *

The most interesting cases involving the cards are extremely subtle. Rosa admitted she had problems—she was on the verge of a divorce and since she had never really had to fend for herself during her early life, she was apprehensive about the tough world of work, jobs, security.

I set out three cards for her past, in the spread I have evolved for my own use. Usually these three cards will give me a basic over-all view of my sitter's early life, generally their childhood until perhaps ten or twelve. By this age, as I explain to them, the character has usually been formed and the child has adopted its perceptions of life, what it sees as reality. This affects the way the person will tackle its journey into adulthood, carrying with it any damage or distortion that has not been dealt with. As any dabbler in psychology is aware, we so often repeat the mistakes we have made in the past, and so this basis of a sitter's background is important, since it might explain a lot of what is wrong in the sitter's 'present' and how they should tackle their future.

Rosa's background cards indicated to me a preoccupation with the men in her life.

'Was your father someone you idolized?' I asked.

'I—didn't have one I knew. But I certainly didn't idolize my step-father. He was rather awful.'

'This card shows me a man who regards himself as the star of the show, the hero. I think it probably represents an idealized picture of your father, as you wanted him to be or think he was.'

'Not consciously,' she said.

'Perhaps not consciously, but we'll start with that as some sort of distorted view of either your father or the male sex. I have the centre card here showing me your mother who seems to have carried around her a heavy dark burden that overshadowed her life— something inexplicable and mysterious.'

She nodded quick agreement. 'Yes, I've never understood how, or what.'

'She passed it on to you, I think, and you get depressed sometimes.'

'Yes, yes,' she said eagerly.

'You feel you are held back, as she was. Probably her mother too—this is a syndrome which is passed down from mother to daughter often.'

'Not held back, but as though there is something blocking the way, and just no way I can go forward. A barrier.'

'Your third card is an older man, perhaps your step-father.'

'My husband,' she said.

'Yes, probably, for I feel you headed for a father-type figure, for security. Going back to the first card, you have brothers, I think. Did you feel they were better treated than you? More important?'

'Well, they were stepbrothers, but yes, I felt as though my mother thought so.'

I laid out the three cards for the 'present'.

'I see here in your central card that you need some form of counselling, unravelling connected with your background and the difficulties it has left you with emotionally. Have you considered any type of counselling?'

'Yes, I have actually been thinking about it,

only recently,' she said.

'Especially in view of your failed marriage. Is there someone else involved?'

She hesitated for a moment. 'Well, yes, there is someone.'

'Can you tell me his first name?'

A slight pause. 'It's her, actually.'

'Oh, I see.'

'It's Morag. She rejected me, though. She sent me a letter after I—well approached her, but I don't know whether she really means no or not.'

When I probed further, I began to see far more complicated patterns form through the cards. I told Rosa:

'There are two pictures here connected with anguish, upset, pain. One is your husband. Even though the marriage was of convenience only, he recognizes your strength and does not want you to leave. The other card is yourself. You seem to be a victim, your future uncertain, more or less alone, very lonely. But there is a second picture here in the "future" spread which indicates to me that you in fact have another side to you and you are very much in control, you do all the manipulating of events and people to suit yourself and achieve the effects you want—or at least, the effects you think should happen.

'Link up with the picture of your mother, your concept of the feminine role as suffering, your ideas about the male sex—these form the

171

basis of your expectations of what life will be like for you. And what you think it ought to be like.'

She was listening intently.

'I am also getting the impression that you are not sure whether it is men or women—or both—or neither—to whom you are drawn. You need to clarify this. You have not really had a healthy relationship with a man or a woman have you, in spite of your various experiences and marriage?'

'No,' she said.

'Counselling will help here, too. But I can tell you one thing. You are a very strong person, and your strength is going to bring you safely through the problems you see ahead. You need a job and it will find you a very unusual job— something to do with security, I think—where you will work more or less alone and travel all over Britain and be up against tough men. You'll win hands down. And you are going to be able to take your pick of the partners— potential partners—whatever you decide— that you want.'

*   *   *

One of the subtlest things about the cards is that quite often, they will volunteer the information that the sitter has some sort of so-called sexual 'deviation', generally very unexpectedly and when I am not looking for

172

anything along these lines. If I feel the information can be helpfully used to assist the sitter, I mention it, usually in a vague and unspecific way, simply pointing out that there is no reason to feel ashamed if one does not seem to go along with 'ordinary' attitudes towards sex. I usually suggest that they may find themselves feeling their sexual interests are something they are reluctant to admit to but so long as they are with a partner who can participate and enjoy their pleasure, and no one is being hurt, I tell them to go ahead and make sure they enjoy themselves.

The cards deal specifically with the past, present and future, and may also concentrate on one particular aspect of a sitter's life—business, relationships, success in different spheres. Health and wealth too reveal what they hold in store. And specific questions can be answered with a 'yes' or 'no' by cutting the cards.

These are typical examples of snatches of cases where the secrets have indeed been 'written' in the layout of the cards.

*　　　*　　　*

Madge, willowy and blonde, well-preserved and exquisitely dressed and attractive even though she is no longer young. I lay out the cards for her 'past'.

The cards themselves do not matter in my

case, since as I have explained, I work clairvoyantly from the pictures and images I see rather than the traditional significance of each card. And the pictures I am seeing here are, alas, far too often repeated.

I take Madge's hands.

'You're very tense under all the glitz, aren't you?' I say. 'And the reason why is here. Madge, you had a ghastly childhood. You were abused—probably by more than one man. It went on for a long time and you have never told anyone or come to terms with it. You have tried to feel you value yourself, and you count, and you matter—but this terrible experience has been with you always, and overshadowed every thing you have done, every relationship you have had.'

Madge's friend, who is sitting with her, gives her a startled look, but the answer is in Madge's face. Tears have come to her eyes and her expression is that of a wounded animal, darkly painful and bewildered.

'Karen doesn't know. Nobody has ever known—you're quite right,' she says very quietly. 'It—I have never spoken about it. But you are right. It was—as bad as you say, and it went on for years. There were three apart from my father—two brothers and an uncle.'

Her friend, horrified, makes to protest, but she gives a small grimace.

'Yes, now you know. It happened.'

'And now that you have broken your silence,

you can start to cope,' I tell her. 'All these years have been ruined by what was done to you. Do you want the rest of your life to be ruined too? Give them a total victory?'

Unexpectedly, she wipes away her tears with a determined movement.

'No, I'm glad you brought it out. I'm glad you know, Karen. The relief—I couldn't do it myself, but I'm glad somebody did it for me. I've lived with it long enough, I want to learn to let it go.'

*   *   *

Such positivity often results from what the cards reveal about the past. If the sitter is not able to see how to overcome the ghosts which can stalk us through life, I am able to assist him or her to proceed in the right direction. Al waited for me to lay out the three cards for his past, and again this was a past which I have seen often in varying degrees.

'I'm afraid you had a lonely childhood. I would say you went to public school—?' He nodded. 'Probably to preparatory school as well from a very early age, and the rejection, or sense of rejection is something you have felt very keenly ever since. Difficulties in relating to other people—you felt you had little love or affection from your parents, and I think your father criticized you. Maybe the situation was not quite as drastic as this, but it was how you,

175

as a child, perceived things. You have been ultra-sensitive ever since, and critical of yourself. Are you in a relationship at the moment?'

He nodded. 'I would guess that you are the one who gives—your partner is the one who takes. Right?'

A half-smile and shrug. 'I suppose you could say that. Yes, it's quite true actually. He—Mike—is younger than me, and I indulge him. He isn't always easy to please.'

'You will always do this so long as you feel you cannot risk rejection, and have such a low opinion of yourself,' I said. 'I see here in the present the evidence of solid success at work, in business. You will never be a poor man. You are very astute in most ways, it's only with regard to your relationships that this unhappy background and the loneliness of your private self cripples you.'

*   *   *

Other situations I come across in the 'past' cards are like that of Katrin.

'You went without—materially at any rate—you had next to nothing. Family broken up too, a very deprived background. But in spite of that, your childhood was happy, and you related to nature. You saw goodness and loveliness everywhere. You discovered books and escaped into reading and found your own

176

ways of being content. In the middle of nothing, you were surrounded by riches.'

Smiling, she nods, and I tell her: 'All those riches have been with you as you grew, and will be with you always. And you are a person who gives, you shower gifts on everyone you meet, everyone you know.'

*   *   *

The cards for the present often help to make the situation clear. Ursula had told me she wanted to leave her husband, and asked for advice as to the best way to go about it and proceed with a divorce, but when I laid out the cards for the present, I saw that all three of her cards were concerned with her husband and her relationship to him. There was nothing about her own wishes or activities, nor her children, nor the other man she had mentioned as her lover.

'I think that, whatever you might imagine you want, you are very much connected to your husband, and would find it difficult to leave him—if indeed you really want to. From these cards it appears your whole life revolves round him. I am sensing that you want to hurt him because you are jealous—he has withdrawn from you, I think—or you feel he has, and you resent the time he spends with other people or at work. Is he having problems with his work?'

'Well, yes,' she agreed reluctantly. 'He does work late often—and things—well aren't the same as they were.'

'Maybe the difficulty is that he has grown into his responsibilities and you are still waiting, like a child, for the romance and magic to come back,' I said. 'Be honest, I don't think you really care about this lover at all, do you? Can you seriously tell me you want to spend the rest of your life with him? Compared to your husband he is just what Shakespeare might refer to as a "callow youth". You respect your husband—you secretly despise this other man, particularly because you can manipulate and control him. Right?'

She twisted her hands then looked up candidly. 'Yes. 'Fraid so.'

'If you face up to your real motives you will take the right path forward,' I told her. 'You would, I think, commit the most dreadful mistake if you went off with this other man or actually started proceedings to divorce your husband. You have to try and talk things through, to learn to accept your husband as he is and your situation as it is not as you wish it could be.' I laid out cards for her future.

'It seems to me that your husband will probably meet you halfway and be glad of your support and encouragement. He comes across as very tired, he is carrying a lot on his own and although he has no time to try and work out why things have gone wrong, it has upset him

178

too. He feels he is losing you and he has no idea why. He is also proud and, I think, doesn't express himself easily.'

She nodded.

'Well, it's up to you to either mend the situation or lose what you have altogether.'

I explained to her, as I do to most sitters, that even the tarot cards do not categorically dictate 'what the future will hold', rather they point out potential paths that can be taken, or the best ways in which the desires of the sitter can be happily and successfully achieved.

There are in fact many alternative futures, and it is by becoming aware of the possibilities and potentials as revealed in the cards that the sitters can leave their sessions armed with the ammunition to make the right choices and proceed in the directions which will bring about the futures they wish for and desire.

*   *   *

Often, though the cards can be amazingly specific. Dana, a statuesque brunette, with incredibly blue eyes, was working at a mundane temp job, at a loss as to how her life would proceed. I laid out the cards for her future.

'You will get a well-paid job quite soon, and with, or through a powerful woman who seems to be in charge of her own business. You will meet a man—seemingly through this job—

who will mean everything to you. He will be very demanding but you will adore him. He will be wealthy, probably at the top of the tree in his profession, and you will travel the world with him and have two homes in different countries.'

I elaborated further on this incredible relationship but secretly I wondered, as she very audibly did, how these things could happen to an ordinary temp. However, within about six weeks, she came to see me again.

'It's happened,' she said. 'At least, I think it has. I have been offered a job by a powerful and wealthy woman, the pay is incredible. I want to know whether I should take it. It was a friend who sort of introduced me so I think it must be all right.'

Further investigation revealed that the job was with a reputable escort agency, which did not surprise me as Dana's figure, face and sapphire eyes were stunning and I thought she would do very well. In fact, I told her, this explained how she would meet the charismatic love of her life. Through the agency.

'A man like that? He wouldn't—would he?' she asked, obviously disappointed.

'Maybe he's tired from travelling and needs to relax, he doesn't have many people close to him, he might just need a pleasant person to talk to and one of his staff sends for a lovely, elegant woman to have dinner with him,' I suggested. 'Anything's possible. But you will

180

meet him.' The first part of the prediction happened very quickly. I am still waiting to hear how the rest of it turns out.

*   *   *

When asking questions via the cards, sitters often want to know if they will 'be wealthy' or 'be successful and make a lot of money.' Generally however, the psychic powers are very chary of being specific about money and material riches. I cannot, for instance, predict winners of races or winning lines for football pools, and I have never met a psychic who makes a serious claim to be able to do this.

The reason seems to be because the higher one rises in psychic awareness, the more one 'lets go' of the material riches and turns to the riches of the spirit—peace of mind, contentment, harmony and balance in living, selflessness rather than selfishness, giving rather than trying to find something for nothing.

The cards do not take kindly, either, to petty or trivial questions being asked, and anyone who persists in forcing the issue over queries which are unnecessary and could probably be answered by common sense, find that the powers simply dry up—temporarily at least—and no answers are given. This is another example of the powers being withdrawn if they are not being wisely used.

CHAPTER TEN

ACHIEVEMENT

Martha, leaning forward intently with her blonde hair shining.

'It is Victorian England and children were exploited. You were a little boy, a sort of Oliver Twist type, and you were one of those who were sent up the chimneys of big houses.'

She nods, her eyes beginning to glisten with tears.

'You were a frail child, you did it because you had no choice, and your life was struggle and darkness. In the end, as happened to many of these children, you just did not come back out of the great warren of chimneys. You were trapped—it wasn't that you'd grown too big, but you were just trapped in a difficult bit, and hadn't got the strength to move. And you died there.'

It is well into Martha's session, and her initial tough sophistication has been faced with several past lives where she was used and exploited.

'All of this is still with you,' I say. 'Even though you are successful, have fought your way through in this life, those frail children who did not understand, who simply endured the dark and did not understand joy or delight or the pleasure of just being, haunt you all the time, and stop you from letting go and enjoying the pleasure of what you have and what you have done.'

Wordlessly, her eyes still glittering with unshed tears, holding my hands tightly, she nods again. She does not look at me.

'It's time to put the burden down, Martha,' I tell her gently. 'You don't need to carry their pain and torment any more. You can set that little boy in the chimney free from his dark prison. He's just old bones crumbling in with even older stones and soot and fears that don't matter any longer. You can set his spirit free to play in green fields with the sun on his face, and he can learn to laugh and run and—what do you think he would have liked? A white pony maybe—something trusting and more helpless than himself. Set them all free and you will be able to go forward from today without that heavy load of their sorrows weighing you down.'

'It's true,' she says in a small voice. 'However I struggle, I never seem to be getting anywhere. And even when I look at my achievements—I *am* successful, with my own business, and I know I can look the part, look good and attract men.' She shakes her head helplessly. 'It seems to be without a point, as though everything turns to ashes, sort of. As though I should be dealing with much more important problems, if only I knew what they were.'

'You have been carrying the sufferings and deaths of these children, unable to soothe their fear or wipe away their tears. We can set them free now, so that in the knowledge that you have sent them into the keeping of those who will care for them, and laid their little spirits to rest, you can look at yourself clearly, as you really are, without their pain and misery blinding your vision. Your lesson for this life is to learn to enjoy living, to be able to give to others not by solving the terrible problems of misery and suffering but by being a happy, warm and shining woman who makes life more pleasant for others by her own positive qualities and inspiration. Because you will have fought a great battle, you will have found strength that other people can draw on. Does this make sense to you?'

Her eyes are shining now with different tears, and she is holding her head high.

'It's impossible to tell you the lightness I feel, to have found an answer. I feel I have been looking all my life for this. I want the children to have their pony and the green field, and I know they will be safe now.' She breaks down suddenly, sobbing, and dabs at her eyes. 'I can't tell you—the relief—I know things will be all right now.'

*   *   *

Jeanie is a lady of great sweetness, greying hair

loose round her shoulders, her wide eyes brave in the face of the greatest emptiness a woman can know.

'I have just lost my husband,' she tells me softly. 'I don't think I can live without him.'

We are forced to conduct her sitting in the busy cafeteria of the building where I would normally have been working in a private room. She takes my hands across the cafeteria table trustingly, like a child, ignoring the background of inappropriate noise—and yet, in many ways more fitting than solemn music, for death is just as much a part of life as families ordering eggs and chips, and 'a small portion for the little girl'.

I pick up her husband.

'He was younger than you. Good looking. Hair—in a pony tail?'

'Twenty years younger.' Her hands are holding on tightly, her tears are flowing freely from those wide blue eyes.

The messages he has for her are simple.

'He found it difficult to express his love, I think. To reveal his feelings.' She nods agreement.

'Yes, I used to feel I showed mine too much and it embarrassed him. But now...'

'He wants you to know that he will never leave you. The sun that warms you, the breeze that cools your cheek, the starry night sky and the changing seasons—he will be there when you feel the sun or look up at the stars. He says he could not write this as a poem for you when he was alive, or tell you in words, but this is how much he loved you and what he wanted to give you, and he gives it to you now.'

By the end of the session, Jeanie is shaken and weak with spent emotion, but tells me: 'I feel so much at peace now. I could not bring myself to believe—really believe—but now I know that of course there will be a gaping wound, but I have not lost him, and it is enough simply for me to just—carry on loving him without trying to know all the answers. Just keep loving. I can't tell you what this has done for me. I feel strong, as though I can manage somehow. I really have faith now, faith that he is all right, and that I will come through.'

Just as the session is ending I say: 'I am getting an image of chrysanthemums for you. Does that mean anything?'

Her composure cracks. 'I planted some chrysanthemum plants on his grave this morning.'

'He's saying, thank you,' I tell her, smiling. 'They are lovely. And keep them around you at home, he will be there in the colours and texture of the petals.'

'I will.' She leans over to give me a hug and I hold her tightly.

'Thank you,' she says, as she straightens up, looking into my eyes. 'You don't know what you have done for me this afternoon.'

'No, not me. Your love and faith and your own courage have done everything. You will be all right now?'

'Yes,' she says steadily. 'I will be all right— now.'

*   *   *

All psychics are different and I have found that the sitters who are drawn to me are often people who are at a serious cross-roads in their life, or who have very heavy karmic or emotional or spiritual problems. Much of the work I do is concerned with the possible or the potentially achievable rather than the prosaic day-to-day details of ordinary living.

In difficult situations or at times of very great stress or need, ordinary people find they are having to draw on reserves of courage, endurance, strength they did not realize they possessed. At times when things are going well the average person is generally not interested in having their cards read or their future foretold—they have the confidence of the present and the conviction that all will be well in the future. In the healing and counselling I do, I try to give sitters this faith—not that nothing bad will happen to them, but that whatever it is, they will have the strength to endure it and come through it safely.

It is through the difficulties, the pain and suffering, that people find their stature and reach their potential as great souls. Everyone (with a few exceptions) whom I have ever encountered as a psychic has shown me they have the potential for greatness, and it is when I have seen them set their face towards a difficult destiny, or accept a burden they feel they cannot carry, with the steady promise that, somehow, they will manage to do it, that I feel I am carrying out the task for which I was granted my powers. As a psychic, I am here to assist sitters who come to me round difficult corners, to reveal themselves to themselves, to show them that they are twice as big as they think they are. It is my task to show them not only that they can reach for the stars, but that they can clasp the stars in one hand and the sun and the moon in the other.

I see the potential of each soul who comes to sit across the table from me. Sometimes, as I have detailed in this book, the time is not right and even the smallest step forward is not possible. In other cases, like that of Marie, (who in six months went from hopeless despair to the prospect of a new love, a new job, a new life) I have witnessed incredible transformations. In the case of Jeanie, lost in grief for her husband, I watched her, in the space of half an hour, become filled with peace and light so that she could go forward accepting the burden of her loss with faith and tranquillity.

In the cases of all those who, like Martha,

have carried sorrows which did not belong in this life, and have allowed troubled spirits to go to rest, I have witnessed my sitters taking the apparently unbelievable on trust, 'suspending their disbelief' and opening themselves to the light in faith that I—and the power working through me—would not fail them. I have done my best for each—and the powers never fail and never end.

The result has been that many of the sitters I have encountered have taken great strides forward in their lives in many ways, physical and spiritual—even mental.

In the case of Kathy, a young black woman, I spread the cards and saw in her past the symptoms I see so often, of deprivation in childhood, lack of love, abuse. I saw too the resulting inability to form satisfactory relationships, the drifting from man to man, the suffering from what would be classed as 'sex abuse'. I told her all the details, the fact that she could not say no, that she did not even enjoy sex, the whole pitiful scenario.

'Have you had any treatment for this?' I asked and she shook her head.

'What sort of treatment? I mean, how could I even tell anybody what is wrong?'

'Believe me, if you go to a counsellor, you won't have to explain it. They will know about it,' I told her. 'You're not alone, Kathy, but this is something as bad for you as—as being any other sort of addict, of drinking or bingeing on food or even taking drugs. It's all basically because you have this hole inside, where the love and care should have been, and it was never filled, and you keep trying to fill it. I know that's oversimplifying the situation, but do you see what I mean?'

Very slowly, she inclined her head.

'If you take no action, just go on as you have been doing, and disregard what I have said, that's up to you,' I went on. 'You have the choice. But I want to emphasize that you have an illness—not exactly a mental illness, but an emotional problem—and if you do nothing about it, it will continue to hurt you and will spoil your chances of being happier in the future.' (She had already agreed when I told her she was probably depressed at least part of the time.)

I wrote down the names of books she could consult and urged her again to seek counselling, suggesting various places she could try. And to soothe her fears about how to explain her problem, I also made a list for her of the symptoms which we had discussed, so that she could read them out briefly or show them to the person concerned.

She rose rather hesitantly. I had warned her that it was not an easy step to take, and that she would need to break the conditioning of a lifetime but that if she wanted to throw off the burden of manipulation by others, and gain control of her life and her future, this was something that needed to be done. Her problem—emotional and behavioural—would not go away.

'Good luck, and if you do decide to see someone—I am sure it will work out,' I told her. 'You can do it.'

She was a controlled person not given to extravagant emotion, but she smiled.

'Thank you. I think—I think perhaps I can.'

*   *   *

In a similar type of situation, Sylvie, aged seventeen, sat down looking like a child with her cap of elfin blonde hair and widely made-up enormous eyes. She had come to the fair with two middle-aged women I took to be her mother and aunt (rightly, as it happened) and she watched them walk away, leaving her to have her sitting alone, before telling me she wanted to know how she would get on in her new job, which she was starting the next day. But when I looked at her cards I saw serious problems which were far deeper than concern for a new job.

'You have been kept in a prison—smothered—never allowed to be yourself or grow, or do anything on your own initiative. Your mother—is she a single parent?'

'They—weren't married. I don't know who my dad was.'

'She's putting the most enormous pressure

191

on you, and I can see such great anger in you—but I think you're at a point where you feel this job is the last straw and you're ready to just give up. You didn't even choose the job yourself, did you?'

A brief shake of the head.

'What is the job?' I asked.

'Machining—learning to do piece work,' she said very quietly, and I felt a stir of horror.

'Sylvie, you are being destroyed. This is not for you. Have you tried to do anything about your situation, get help to sort things out?'

She shrugged.

'I kept trying to run away when I was small. But this job, it's my last chance—I've got no GCSEs.'

'You could have got them standing on your head,' I told her forthrightly, and saw her smile. 'You're intelligent and quick and you have many talents if only you were given the chance to use them. What do GCSEs matter? You have abilities for organization, practical things, you could cope with people, you're able to rise to a crisis—yes?'

Somewhat surprised, she nodded agreement. 'Well, I think I could.'

'You pick things up quickly. So I feel this whole situation is wrong for you. You need to get away from your mother—to whatever degree.'

We talked for a long time about her options. The most common problem in such cases is finance, where to live and what to live on. Sylvie's mother had instilled in her such a low—almost non-existent—sense of self-value that she was by now sinking in apathetic despair. In addition her mother had denigrated her relationship with her boyfriend—which I told her from the cards was in fact very good for her. She would be able to trust her boyfriend for support and encouragement if she tried to break away into a new life. In addition, she had two women friends in the London area who might be able to help her establish herself.

We worked out a rough plan for her to try and break away in a series of stages, possibly over a year. I also advised her to read the books I had recommended for Kathy, and seek counselling and support.

'You can't do this on your own,' I told Sylvie. 'Or at least, you might try, but it's like major surgery. You need help—all that anger, for instance, which has been building up throughout your life. And the way you view yourself—and trying to change your whole seventeen years of living. You're brave enough, and tough enough, but don't try to carry it all yourself. Get some backing, and some help.'

She left carrying the folded paper where I had written the names of the books and a few notes, as with Kathy, about her personality difficulties, to tell the doctor or counsellor she consulted. She was not emotional either, and made no promises, but I felt that at the very least, I had been there to throw a rope, as it were, to a drowning soul. Often turning-points that can alter a whole life can happen very unspectacularly, and the people who need the most help to make their leap to the stars usually ask for the least.

*   *   *

Sometimes it happens that the great effort the soul needs to make is not the obvious one, and the case of Rick illustrated this most poignantly. He came to me at the end of a psychic fair, when most of the other people taking part had stopped work or left.

'Please,' he begged. 'I have just come back from Bosnia, I'm still carrying the scars. I need help, I need healing.'

It is not always wise to take such comments at their face value, as there are individuals mentioned in later pages who are usually referred to as 'psychic vampires' who can take and take and take energy from the healer but who never actually make any attempt to right their own wrongs. The result can seem as though a person in a dreadful situation is being callously neglected—but those with experience know that it would be the unprotected healer or psychic who would be drained first, and probably require hospital treatment for exhaustion. The 'vampire' never actually goes under, but having exhausted one host, simply moves on to the next.

The more dramatic the plea for help, the more possible it is that the scenario is a 'front' for something else, so I examined Rick very carefully and eventually agreed to give him a sitting. As soon as I took his hands I could feel the terrible stress, the sleepless nights, the shaking and the pushing himself far beyond the apparent limits of physical strain.

'You are worn out—but you know that,' I told him. 'I do feel though that it is not just healing you need. There is something driving you to this, going into a war zone.'

'It was my second visit. And I'm going again in three weeks,' he told me. 'I've been driving convoys, under fire. I have been hit everywhere, I'm covered with scars, and there's a bullet somewhere in my chest. It hurts a lot. But I have to do it.'

'Why?' I asked.

'Why? How the hell do I know? Somebody has to take the food, the medical supplies through. I tell you, I've seen the bodies rotting there, the children.' There were telltale tears in those tough blue eyes. He was gripping my hands so that I thought the bones would break.

'Let's take it quietly for a minute,' I said. 'Just relax.'

'I can't.' It was a flat statement.

'I can explain to you how to do it, how to

breathe, the exercises,' I said.

He shrugged. 'I'll be back there in three weeks. There's no time there for breathing, lady.'

I worked with Rick for over an hour, trying to calm his frantic mania. I also took a tough line and told him I had no sympathy with his condition. He had got himself into it, and it was up to him to sort the problems out.

Problems not of the war and the work he was doing, but the reason why he was throwing himself so pitilessly over and over into the line of fire. He was, I told him, running away. From the ordinary human problems of family, forming loving ties and taking in the simple everyday responsibilities of ordinary living. He was punishing himself, abusing his body by the bullets, mortars, and bombs of a war which gave him an excuse that 'this is something greater than I am', which he could use to justify his 'sacrifice'.

I also took a firm line on his neglect of his physical person, his carelessness over sleep and gentleness towards himself, the fact that he would not accept correct medical treatment for his wounds—there were at least two, including the bullet, which required surgery.

He admitted, as I gave him healing, that he was in touch with higher spirits, that he could tune in to greater planes, that he had all the psychic powers. I responded by pointing out to him that what he lacked was the ability to accept the 'nitty-gritty' of human living. He had to let his arrogance go, settle for the nuts and bolts of being alive and of being who he was, rather than attempting to daub a great mark across history. He was reaching so very casually for the stars, confident he could not only clasp them but do it with far less effort than other, less gigantic mortals.

'You have got to give up being some great macho hero,' I said. 'Face up to your fears of the ordinary, you're running away because you can't take the mundane.'

I made him promise to have the medical attention he needed and to take more care of himself, to consider using his psychic powers to help people in distress, not just his magnificent physique, to try and connect with the 'real world'. He gave me a one-sided smile, flashed his blue eyes and said he would try. As he left, very reluctant to part company, as we had been through a great deal of mental trauma together during the session, I knew he would go back to the firing line—and that his struggle to find himself would take more out of him than the effort of devoting a life to fighting someone else's war would do from anyone else.

*　　*　　*

In essence, the messages of encouragement have been to help my sitters transcend themselves, to allow their horizons to expand

197

and to try to encompass possible heavens as well as the hells of human existence. Two cases which occurred within days of each other seemed to me to ram the message home from opposite angles. One was that of Raymond, whose past life regressions included one where he had been some sort of missionary or minister who had taken his particular creed to the 'heathen', quite certain within himself that his gospel, narrow and extreme as it was, was the only one.

I saw him being propelled by canoe or small boat in waters which seemed to be somewhere in the southern hemisphere, probably New Guinea or Borneo. He was sitting in a dark cloth coat, a book which I took to be his own particular testament tucked under his arm as though it was his ammunition for a war, staring straight ahead as the boat glided across the water. I seemed to be viewing it pass from the bank, through trailing creeper-like vegetation.

In that life, Raymond had been a relentless bigot, who had repeatedly imposed his views on everyone, including the 'heathen', from his own sense of omnipotence which he would never have dreamed for a moment of questioning, doubting or considering. He had no conception of doing things for other people's benefit, but simply because he knew he was always right.

His bigotry and inflexible egotism met an

equally inflexible end, however, though thankfully I did not view any more details of the incident apart from the boat gliding past the bank. But his intended 'victims' in this case had been cannibals—and they had not tried to argue with him, but had simply eaten him! Raymond and I agreed on reflection that they had probably found him extremely indigestible—difficult to the end.

*   *   *

Roz's message from her past lives also involved the ultimate in survival. I picked her up first as 'Lucy', the inmate of an eighteenth-century asylum, who was so utterly withdrawn into herself that she remembered nothing of who had put her there, and responded to nothing. Though only about eighteen years old, she was emotionally dead from her betrayal by people she had thought loved her, and her physical death was to come soon from consumption.

Further on, after other lives fraught with anxiety and loss, I found that Roz had been a young oarsman, possibly a slave, on a ship round about the time of Christ. It had gone down on rocks near a wild strip of coast with no means of supporting life, just stones and boulders. There had been two or three other survivors, but in the fight for life, they had killed each other, and, sinking into increasing madness, Roz's previous self had found there was no way of survival except to scratch long strips from the bodies of his former companions with his fingernails, chew them and suck stones in place of water. He had died lingeringly of starvation, thirst and raging insanity from the horror of it all.

I wrote on Roz's notes: 'There has been a difficulty in relating to the harshness of life and a tendency to retreat into the mind. Learn to accept being alone, relying on your own strength and try to work on making negative situations positive.'

*   *   *

As a psychic, my sitters have shown me that anything is possible, and I have learned never to be surprised. There is always some unexpected and wonderful new dimension which will reveal itself when the time is right.

Jody had almost finished her reading when she asked whether I could contact her mother—but the spirit which came through was a cheerful black lady back home in Jamaica, who offered her vigorous encouragement and wanted to pour her a drink of some sort of local brew.

Jody smiled. 'It's my grandma.'

I passed their conversation from one to another, her grandma continuing to encourage Jody to be positive with her problems, and when they had finished their chat, I said, as

I always do, that I was going to send the spirit back. I closed my eyes and concentrated on doing this.

I am clairvoyant but not clairaudient (I do not 'hear' actual voices or sounds) and the messages I receive are all, as I have explained, in the form of patterns or shapes which I have to translate. But to my amazement, as grandma set off back to her own realm, I was certain I was picking up a melodious and very catchy rendering of a negro spiritual wafting back to me, as though on some sort of breeze.

'Did your grandma sing?' I asked Jody, dumbfounded.

'Sing—yes, she sang.'

No doubt about it. To my wonder and delight, grandma was just getting into her stride as she left and I watched her safely home, her voice deep and full of joy.

Oh, dem golden slippers,
Oh, dem golden slippers,
Golden slippers I'm goin' to wear
Because dey look so neat.

Oh, dem golden slippers,
Oh, dem golden slippers,
Golden slippers I'm goin' to wear
To walk the golden street.

SORCERER'S APPRENTICES
A Brief Guide for New and Aspiring Psychics

All psychics have to start somewhere, and in most cases it is the experience of a lifetime which gives the psychic gifts their added strength and power. Psychics can 'find themselves' in many ways, at many different ages, according to each individual. There is no 'right' way to become a psychic, nor any infallible method which can ensure 'success'. I have had many cases of 'new' psychics coming to me—being drawn because the time was right—and turning to me for guidance and instruction.

Many are unsure of themselves, their gifts and powers, or they say deprecatingly when I ask, after taking their hands, whether they are psychic: 'Well, I've been told that I am'. Sometimes, as in the case of Jane, whose psychic power came across very strongly, they do not want to acknowledge it exists. I had already picked that up from her hands, and told her: 'The powers are there but they are not being used. You want to ignore them, I think.'

'Yes, I do,' she said flatly. 'I have no desire at all to go messing around with spirits and things. I live a busy life and I haven't got time for all that nonsense.'

'There is no reason why you should take any

notice of them, then, if that is how you feel,' I said. 'But the time might well come when you will feel differently. There is a right time for us all—for you it is not now, but I would ask you to be aware that the powers are there so that you can do what you need to when that time comes.'

She departed declaring ungraciously that 'that time would be never so far as she was concerned.'

From the cases in this book we can see that there are far more potential psychics around than might be thought, far more strange happenings and miracles, far more possibilities for communication and interaction outside our 'ordinary' existence. So it comes as no surprise that other 'new' psychics have been aware since childhood that they had powers and abilities which were out of the ordinary.

Many speak of visions and premonitions that frightened them or that they accepted as normal, but which disturbed their immediate family and caused them to keep further revelations to themselves. When I pick up on their powers and encourage them to be positive about their gifts and have confidence in them, they seem to bloom and are quick to want to talk about their experiences and ask for guidance and advice on how to emerge from the 'closet'.

Then there are sitters like Diane, who sat down and told me directly, flushing in her earnestness:

'I need help. I know I am psychic, and I am doing as much as I can to help myself progress. I read, I meditate, I'm investigating the use of candles and gems and colours and I think I am developing spiritually. But I have nowhere else to go, nobody to ask what to do. What is the next step?'

The new psychic is bewildered because, as I have said, there is no 'next step' as such. Each individual develops at his or her own pace, in the way that is right for them. And what many potential psychics do not realize is that it is not some sort of physical training or activity, working hard at your talent, as it were, which is needed. The psychic powers are not based on some sort of mysterious secret knowledge that has to be studied and learned, with a test at the end to qualify and prove the standards have been upheld.

There are old traditions of the 'fortune-teller' type which still linger, and still give psychics the taint of 'crossing the palm with silver' or else facing the 'gypsy's curse', inevitably representing itself as some sort of con-man rip-off. Some practitioners claim to have had their gifts passed down to them, and are often inclined to rest on their laurels, as it were, seemingly feeling that what has been passed on to them is enough. But being a psychic is a way of life, a discipline of mind as well as body. It is the acquiring of development of inner perception and control which is aimed towards the spiritual rather than the physical, towards a letting go rather than an acquisition of material things.

*   *   *

Many would-be psychics, however, are only marginally interested in the dedication and the discipline. They want to be able to astound their sitters and to be recognized for their abilities—to have lists of important heads (preferably crowned) lining up for bookings. And it is a fact that this type of success can, with a little thought and application, be achieved. Courses which teach tarot card reading, aromatherapy, reflexology, the use of crystals, palmistry and astrology, can be successfully completed and put into practice by people who have no psychic powers at all. Follow the rules in such cases and you will get the results—psychic powers need not enter into it.

There is room in psychic circles for almost every type of practitioner, including those who are not remotely psychic. What people believe, where their powers come from, what they can achieve—their spiritual standing, as it were—is what I regard as their 'private' face, a matter for themselves and the spirits they serve or do not serve. So long as they do not claim powers they do not possess, everyone can in different ways cater for needs. Often, too much clairvoyant power can upset a sitter whose need is for far less.

Paulette was one such sitter who put me in a difficult position in this respect. I was attempting to discuss the impact of her childhood on her personality, as revealed in her cards, and how she was unable to face up to real life, but followed fantasy images and rainbows, with the result that her real life relationships and activities were suffering. I found that because of this very tendency, and because she was not ready to try to come to terms with herself, it was almost impossible to communicate with her, though I sensed her great need of encouragement and reassurance. She desperately wanted to feel that wonderful things were in store, including a potential husband, since all her romantic affairs had gone wrong for the very reason the cards were stating so clearly—her inability to accept reality and real people.

I might have closed the sitting and told her I was unable to give her a reading, but instead, following advice clairvoyantly myself, I explained that her husband-to-be was in Scotland and, if she wanted to find him, she must travel north. She had to make the effort, I said, the fates were not going to do all the work themselves. She had to meet her destiny half way.

She was thrilled and asked for all sorts of

details including his height and build, hair and eye colour, occupation, whether he had ever been in love before, and (on hearing he was waiting for her and had never been serious about any other girl), whether he had actually had sexual experience or was a virgin (she was not too happy about this as a prospect).

The spirits gave me answers to all these questions, and I directed her on where to go in Scotland, on what she should wear and where she was most likely to meet up with him. Their future lifestyle too was discussed in detail. Thrilled and uplifted, she rose to leave, still unaware of the real message I had been given for her, which was that her perceptions of reality were spoiling her life. I felt I had given her a placebo, which would come to nothing. Yet, as with the case of Sara and her Sir Lancelot, if I had heard from Paulette later that she had indeed gone to Scotland and met the man I had described in the place where I had told her she would meet him, I would not have been in the least surprised.

*　　*　　*

People who come to me with psychic powers and seek advice as to how to proceed, are generally concerned with this 'private' side, involving linking in to what they personally believe in and what they think the powers represent, learning how to control those powers so that they can put them to the best and most rightful use. All such power is given to be used for the benefit of others, and not for oneself. Until these basic disciplines are accepted the psychic will not develop.

Spiritual advancement, though, has to be studied in far greater detail than through one sitting with me. I usually recommend the most important thing as trying to contact and keep in contact with similarly minded and gifted people, who will at least talk the same language and give the new psychic support and encouragement. The most reputable and easiest place for most people to contact their own kind is at their local Spiritualist church—names and information will be available there, as well as healing and exchange of views from others who also possess the psychic powers. Some people find themselves in a different 'stream' of belief and activity, but, even if you feel you want to move on, you will have somewhere like a development circle, a gathering of pagans, druids, extraterrestrials or some other branch of 'alternative' belief and psychic activity to move on to. There is a famous saying that: 'When the pupil is ready the teacher will appear.'

*   *   *

An important point which must be mentioned was brought up by Deirdre when she consulted me. She was tense and nervous, and I asked her what was causing her fear. We had already established that she was psychic and wanted to work with her powers.

'Well, this friend of mine—a sort of friend—she's a medium and she told me that you can get into all sorts of trouble if you don't protect yourself—spiritually I mean—against the bad spirits that can get to you—and you might even think they are good ones. You might hear things and you might believe they're coming from the light, but they're really from the devil. How can I protect myself?'

On other occasions I have been told as I was with an off-hand Shannon (as well as in the tragic case of Charmaine and her devil-dedicated son): 'I had some bad experiences when I was younger—messing around with the ouija board. It was quite frightening, but I'm all right now.'

*   *   *

The main point is that these 'bad experiences' can happen and they can be so severe that inexperienced people can be frightened beyond the realms of sanity and may need great care and a long time to recover. They occur mainly when the psychic powers and all they stand for are treated by the uninitiated as a joke, a game, or something they want to meddle with out of daring or inquisitiveness, idle or malicious curiosity, 'just to see what happens'. Or when greed for power rears its ugly head. In all ignorance the damage will mainly be done, but once it has been done it cannot be retracted. So even if you think you are psychic, make sure always that you know what you are doing, and if you are not sure, don't attempt psychic activities without the company of someone else, preferably someone more experienced.

If you have no real idea of what you are doing then DO NOT DO IT. All psychics have learned their skills via a hard road of experience and had to face up to malicious and terrifying situations. 'Psychic attacks' for instance, which can take the form of a sort of 'tornado' of negative energy that can cause illness, incapacity and extreme fear, are just one example of the hazards psychics need to learn to cope with. They become very familiar, too, with the 'psychic vampire', which drains its host of all energy.

My own personal test—unrecognised for what it was at the time—came when I was aged about eight, and I had to face the devil, his henchmen and a gigantic army of demons. I knew I must stand my ground against the terror or I would be lost, and somehow I must have done it, but fear like this can kill. The psychic learns how to cope with it however, and how to develop strength so that he can protect himself and others against further attacks. But the inexperienced meddler, who does not appreciate the power he is messing about with, can do very great damage both to himself and to others.

*   *   *

When setting out on your path as a psychic, the one basic rule to follow in order to protect yourself against all evil and negativity is to invoke the white light of good, of the Spirit, God—whatever you wish to call the source of positivity and power—and mentally drench yourself in it, so that the white light pervades every part of you. Everything that is selfless, loving, positive, is of the light; anything which provokes negativity or selfish preoccupations comes from somewhere else and should be avoided. This is a quick way to gauge whether your inspirations and visions are coming from the right place.

You may also be taught to 'open and close' the chakras—the energy points of the body—or other methods intended to protect.

But basically, it is fear itself that breeds the monsters. If your belief in the power of the light, the Spirit, God, or your vision of good in whatever form, is utter and complete, you will know there is nothing to fear since whatever you come up against will be a projection of your own negativity and you will be given strength and the weapons to cope with it. But since we are human, most of us do not possess that sort of faith, and so we have our own particular fears. When we think of the dangers of modern living, raping, mugging, drugs, car accidents, any type of phobia, or whatever we fear, it will vary with each of us since our own individual demon will take the form of our own especial fear.

*   *   *

One of the tasks a psychic must learn is to help protect sitters, not so that their fears will go away but so that they can learn to cope with them. Consequently, a psychic has to project an image of strength, wisdom and capability. Psychic fairs are based largely on the premise that it is far better to allow a visitor to look round and choose the person they feel drawn to rather than directing incomers towards the medium, the clairvoyant or the tarot reader who happens to be free just then, even if the visitor chooses to bypass ten readers who are free and join a long queue for someone else who is quite obviously going to be busy for several hours.

When you become a psychic, you are offering your own particular powers and gifts to be of assistance. Some people will find that they're drawn to what you have to offer and have confidence in you, others will not. Even your name can make a difference so you must present yourself carefully.

212

A psychic can work with nothing but his mind to draw on, but there are certain rituals and ingredients which help to make a sitting far more pleasant and meaningful for both sides. For instance, the sitting is nearly always conducted as just that—a 'sitting', where the participants are seated close to each other, generally with the psychic's table between them. On this table the psychic sets out the 'tools of the trade', which comprise their own particular focuses for their power, their cards and crystals or stones, the symbols of their own special 'god'—some, for instance, are drawn to Egyptian symbolism and may have a cat (the Ancient Egyptian goddess Bastet) or a head of Nefertiti or the Sphinx to give them inspiration.

Prevalent on most tables, which are decorated with rich cloths, often glittering with silver or gold or in the purple colours of power (amethyst is the stone of majesty and strength) the psychic will place their cards and their crystal ball. The beautiful decorations of the tables are, in the same way that the tarot cards are wrapped in a silk cloth, to show that the psychic values the power he or she has been given as beyond price, and therefore treats it with respect and deference.

Again on most tables are flowers and candles. Apart from being pleasing, these

213

provide links with the earth and the powers of nature and the candle flames signify both light and the gift of fire, which are purifying in psychic terms.

Crystals and gem-stones are used symbolically and also for their calming and soothing properties as they lie or stand on the psychic's table. The most popular are plain quartz crystals themselves, which are sources of powerful energy on which the psychic can draw; chunks of the beautiful pink rose quartz which is the stone of love, self-love and self-confidence; clusters of amethyst for power and control; and sometimes boxes containing a 'treasure chest' of many different gem-stones. It is good to have agate about in some form, as it is balancing and healing, as is the lovely green aventurine.

*   *   *

The main problem encountered by new psychics is that they find it difficult to believe in their own powers. Summing this up is the case of Vivienne, with whom I have been working over several months at psychic fairs. I have been appearing in my capacity as a clairvoyant, medium and healer. She sells crystals and candles and other items at a tasteful stall—I soon invested in no fewer than three necklaces of differently clustered garnets from India (garnets signifying 'true love'!).

214

Viv is well aware that she is psychic, and has even experienced the flow of the power through her hands. She has been experimenting with a tarot pack and working on her spiritual development. When I look at her, I can often see the power all around her.

'If you came to the fair next week, not as a stallholder but to work as a psychic, what do you think you would most need to know?' I asked her.

'To just sit there as a psychic? It would be frightening,' she said seriously. 'I think the worst thing is that I can never believe that what I see or feel is really "the thing". I keep asking myself whether I'm imagining it.'

'That happens to everyone at the beginning. It's just a matter of confidence.'

'Well, I suppose I most need the confidence then,' she smiled.

'I think if people were aware of the really weird messages and things that come through—which are absolutely true and real—they would be staggered,' I said. 'I can't think of anything unusual enough, but I have had cases where I have thought to myself, "Oh, I can't possibly say this to my sitter", but then I do, and they respond in the most positive way. Like—for a crazy example—I might say to an imposing lady who looks as though she has spent her life pruning the roses and judging the lightest sponge competition, that I am picking up a naked man jumping up and down in a mud-hole and grunting and to my stupefaction she smiles in genuine delight and says: "Oh, it's so lovely that you've linked up with Daddy; we had such fun during those years in Africa".'

Vivienne laughs, then becomes serious again. 'I think, really,' she says, 'that I would like to know what to expect. Just what I am going to have to face, so that I will be able to manage.'

'That's a very sensible attitude, because in the psychic world, the psychic can be confronted by literally anything. From an angel to a devil, a saint to a soul in hell. You will never really know what to expect, except that there will be people who need you, always. And people who are searching, and think you might have the answers. Sometimes you will have those answers, and the seekers will break down and cry with sheer thankfulness that they have found you. And—amazing in circles where the aim should be to transcend the material world—you will meet a great deal of the mean and miserable and petty who will trip you up and make you doubt yourself and everybody else. There is only one rule really, one way through. Hold fast to the light always. And however naïve or incredible or silly you feel—or get labelled by those around you— cling to the light and what it stands for.'

Viv is thoughtful. 'I suppose it's never going to be easy.'

'The personal fears and doubts never stop.

You need them too, because they prove that you yourself are still growing and moving forward. But a psychic deals in intangibles that can mean life to one person and absolutely nothing to another. Greater people than myself have questioned the nature of trust, faith, love. Don't try to apply logic or rational laws. The psychic world has its own rules.'

I smile at Viv.

'You just have to be prepared to believe in your powers—however you yourself personally visualize the positive nature of their source—and be there, be ready. For whatever you encounter. Ask for guidance. If you are holding to the light, to positivity and selflessness and the fact that you are an instrument for the greater benefit of others—in whatever way that light sees fit—you will always be given whatever is necessary. Not what you—or they—might ask for or want, but what is necessary. Whatever you need will be supplied. The rest we each of us have to do for ourselves.'

SELECTED BOOKS
RECOMMENDED TO SITTERS

Berne, Eric, *Games People Play* (André
   Deutsch, London, 1966)
Bradshaw, John, *Homecoming—Reclaiming
   and Championing Your Inner Child*
   (Piatkus, London, 1991)
Cunningham, *Wicca: A Guide for the Solitary
   Practitioner* (Llewellyn, St Paul,
   Minnesota, 1989)
Harris, Thomas A., *I'm OK—You're OK*
   (Pan, London 1973)
Jampolsky M.D., Gerald G., *Love is Letting
   Go of Fear* (Celestial Arts, Berkeley,
   California, 1979)
Jeffers, Susan, *Feel the Fear—And Do it
   Anyway* (Century Hutchinson, London,
   1987)
The Bible
The Koran

also:

Gater, Dilys, *Zodiac* [short stories with
   astrological commentary by Richard
   Lawler] (forthcoming from Ulverscroft)
Lawler, Richard, *Secrets of the Tarot Cards*
   (forthcoming from Ulverscroft)